Tim,

It has been a pleasure knowing you. Hope we can work more together in the future.

Best of Luck!

Jeff Slusser

ACQUIRING PROFIT

*The Win/Win System to Real Estate
Mergers and Acquisitions*

George Slusser
with Warren Berger

Foreword by Tom Dooley, CEO, North American Consulting Group

Copyright ©1995 Electronic Realty Associates, L.P.
ISBN 0-9649100-0-4
Library of Congress Catalog Card Number: 95-90767

All rights reserved. No part of this publication may be reproduced, stored in a retrieval system, or transmitted, in any form or by any means, electronic, mechanical, photocopying, recording, or otherwise, without the prior written permission of the copyright owner.

Published by Electronic Realty Associates, L.P.

Printed in the U.S.A.

This book is dedicated to:

Van, Kate, Paige, Heather, Nick, and Austin

Our legacy

Table of Contents

Acknowledgements   *v*
Foreword, by Tom Dooley   *vi*

Chapter 1   *Why Buy or Sell a Real Estate Company?*   *1*
Chapter 2   *The Basics*   *21*
Chapter 3   *Getting Started: Identifying Candidates*   *33*
Chapter 4   *Breaking the Ice: Approaching a Candidate*   *45*
Chapter 5   *Relationship Building*   *59*
Chapter 6   *Information Gathering*   *73*
Chapter 7   *Potential Fit and Company Valuation*   *93*
Chapter 8   *Putting the Transaction in Motion*   *115*
Chapter 9   *Closing the Deal*   *135*
Chapter 10   *Making It All Work and Moving Ahead*   *155*

Addendum A & B   *Case Studies*   *165*
Addendum C   *Glossary*   *177*

Acknowledgments

This book would never have been attempted without the best friends and teammates ever assembled; the agents, members, and corporate staff of Team ERA.

There are so many people who have contributed greatly to all of our efforts, I can only say a blanket thank you to the dozens who have helped but I fail to name.

There are two people without whom I can assure you this project would never have approached a publishable quality level. They are Allison Hunter, my tireless and outstanding assistant, and Warren Berger, writer extraordinaire and friend.

The following people contributed greatly with their support, wisdom, insights, and examples: Victor Goulet, Robert Purcell, Mac Heavener, Tom Schmitt, Dick Rafferty, Mario Polo, Dr. Steve Franklin, Stewart Wilson, Chet Hogan, Gloria Frazier, Mark Masters, Ken Ulsaker, Tommy McIntosh, Jim Porter, Brad Rush, Cary Troop, Jr., Dennis Fahey, and Tom Dooley.

I would also like to thank Karan McReynolds for the content design, McNeill Lehman for the cover design and Mary Barton for the production. Also the hundreds of people I have worked with on mergers and acquisitions that provided the real experiences and testing ground from which the material was gathered.

Finally I want to thank three very important people to me, my parents Lawrence and Jean Slusser and my wife and best friend, June. Without their inspiration, guidance, and "is it done yet?" this effort could not have been completed.

Thank you all.

Foreword

By Tom Dooley, CEO
North American Consulting Group

Need anyone remind real estate people that they live and work in a world of constant change? That's never been truer than it is today. Dynamic transformations are happening all around us.

One such transformation involves the dramatic increase in the number of mergers and acquisitions taking place in our business. It is increasingly common for individual real estate firms — be they large, small or in-between — to expand and contract by joining forces with another firm or through the buy/sell process.

In fact, changes in ownership of real estate firms has been a major characteristic of the last decade. Many small firms have banded together in an attempt to enhance economies of scale. Mid-sized companies have realized that they're either "too big to be little" or "too little to be big" — and they've responded by selling to another company or expanding their own company through acquisition. Even the large market leaders and megabrokers have not been immune to the trend of changing ownership. Seven of the top 25 brokerage firms in the U.S. in 1988 failed to make a similar list in 1994. The reason: They have been absorbed by other members of the top 25.

There is every indication that the trend toward consolidation in the real estate industry will continue — and perhaps accelerate — as the 21st Century draws nearer. It will be driven by urgent bottom-line needs. In recent years, the profitability of real estate companies has come under siege from a variety of forces — upwardly spiraling commissions to agents, increasing costs of technology, extensive advertising expenditures, and other assaults on the budget. To combat this attack on the bottom line, many progressive real estate firms have resorted to a basic principle: When net margins are low, sustain profitability by increasing gross income. Or, in other words, if the bottom line slips, inflate the top line.

That is often accomplished through expansion — of market share, community presence and gross volume. And in today's world, most brokers contend that the quickest and easiest route to such expansion is through acquisition of other firms. Far better to "buy" than to "make," they assert, especially if the purchase involves a solid operation with a core team of quality agents. Such a successful acquisition can help a broker vault to the next level seemingly overnight.

But the operative word here is "successful" — because if a broker acquires the "wrong" company, or somehow mishandles the delicate process of merging two corporate cultures into one, the result can be the opposite of the intended goal. As author and acquisition expert George Slusser points out in Acquiring Profit, it is as easy for a real estate firm embarking on expansion to "buy failure" as it is to acquire success.

Having presided over more than 100 mergers and acquisitions during his career in the real estate business, Slusser understands the subtle and sometimes precarious art of melding two companies into one. Experience has taught him that when buyer and seller come together, both sides must "win" — otherwise, it is quite likely that both will eventually lose.

There are a great many acquisitions experts in the business world today, but Slusser is a specialist: During his years with Merrill Lynch and for the last 11 years with ERA, Slusser has focused exclusively on acquisitions within the real estate brokerage business. And that is an important distinction. While there are certain universal truths and laws pertaining to any merger and acquisition, regardless of the nature of the business, it's also true that there is a peculiarity to the transfer of ownership of a real estate firm that clearly distinguishes it from most other types of businesses.

Unlike other businesses, the real estate industry does not have widely-recognized established methods of determining the market value of a given firm at a given point in time. The multi-industry

Foreward   vii

barometers of price-earnings, multiple of revenues, assets plus goodwill and cash flow projections are not easily adaptable to a real estate scenario. When such formulas are used in real estate, it is usually in conjunction with some other estimate of worth based on a raft of potential factors, both tangible and intangible.

Because of this complexity, there are few individuals who possess sufficient skill and understanding to merit consideration as merger and acquisition specialists for our particular industry. Pure academic scholars and generic business consultants are usually not up to the task because of their limited perspective on the nuances of the real estate industry. But, on the other hand, few experts at real estate brokerages have the general business and economic overview needed to put a "deal" into a framework suitable for success.

Slusser is one of the few who demonstrates keen competence in both realms. In this book, Slusser conveys the full force of his M&A expertise in a most succinct and articulate manner. While the book is primarily directed toward buyers/acquirers, its sound advice is equally applicable to any real estate owner contemplating a sale or merger. And that includes brokers who may be thinking about a sale five or ten years down the road.

Slusser knows, and conveys to his readers, the important fact that sales of real estate companies are undertaken for a wide variety of reasons, many of them not directly related to financial statements. He realizes, too, that even though the reasons why sellers sell may differ dramatically from the reasons why buyers buy, sellers and buyers need not be at odds with each other.

In fact, a central theme in this book is Slusser's belief — borne out by his experience — that the "win/win" negotiating philosophy, as advocated by some of the more innovative minds in today's business world, happens to be an ideal way to approach real estate mergers and acquisitions. Anyone involved, or soon to be involved, in an acquisition would do well to consider this approach.

In addition to outlining a philosophical approach, Slusser provides a practical, step-by-step roadmap for the would-be acquirer to use in accomplishing a successful transaction. And at each step of the way, the author backs up his recommendations with comments and anecdotes from successful real estate brokers, who agreed to share their acquisition experiences with Slusser and his readers. What these brokers tell us is that the strategies and ideas put forth in this book have been tested in the marketplace. And they really do work. Which is why <u>Acquiring Profit</u> merits a front row spot in a personal real estate library.

Unfortunately, not every real estate acquisition is a successful one. The landscape is dotted with the remnants of ill-conceived mergers or acquisitions where one (or both) of the parties failed to think through the consequences of the transaction and did not plan accordingly. And Slusser himself readily acknowledges that there is no foolproof plan for acquisitions; there will always be a certain level of risk involved. But this book should help those who are embarking on acquisitions to minimize that risk, and to avoid some of the most common pitfalls of the acquisition process. And in so doing, it should help more than a few practitioners to achieve the kind of profitable expansion that is requisite to future success in the rapidly-changing real estate business.

CHAPTER ONE

Why Buy or Sell a Real Estate Company?

A few years ago, real estate broker Dick Rafferty knew his business was at a crossroads. Competition in his local market of Huntington Beach, California, was heating up. Costs of running his single-office company were rising. Rafferty needed to grow — and quickly. He knew that if he didn't, he risked falling behind and becoming unprofitable.

Rafferty could have embarked upon a massive recruitment effort. And he could have opened a new office, from scratch, to house those agents. But Rafferty decided, instead, to acquire an existing company — a longtime competitor — located across town. In one fell swoop, he accomplished the following:

- Gained a team of experienced agents.

- Gained a new business partner (the seller) who had particularly valuable experience at running computer systems; Rafferty's own company was in need of such expertise.

- Extended his company's sales presence to the other side of town — opening up a whole new market for his agents.

- Doubled his company's size and visibility overnight.

- Subsequently was able to get more mileage and greater cost efficiencies out of his advertising, training and other support programs.

"Today," says Rafferty, "we're a much stronger company overall because of the acquisition."

All across the real estate landscape today, more and more brokers are choosing to follow the same path as Rafferty. Mergers and acquisitions have been in the headlines consistently in the last few years. In some cases, these alliances have involved relatively small firms, such as ERA/Rafferty, Lloyd & Associates ($130+ million). But many of the mergers have involved the rapidly growing national franchises or the mid-sized to large independent multi-office brokerages. The trend toward company consolidation caused by the lack of profitability is sweeping across the business — and it is changing the fundamental nature of the real estate business.

As recently as the early 1990's, many successful brokerages could be classified as "mom-and-pop" operations — small, one-office companies with just a handful of agents and a good feel for the local market. But many of those smaller operations have disappeared in recent years. Overall, the industry has seen a decline in the actual number of agents and brokers, and that trend is expected to continue. Statistics from the National Association of Realtors indicate that there are currently about 700,000 real estate agents — and it's projected that by the end of this decade, that number will drop to 500,000 (SEE GRAPH, FIG. 1-A). In terms of real estate companies, we're now down from over 90,000 companies a decade ago to about 70,000 companies — and that number, too, is expected to dip sharply, down to perhaps 50,000 by the end of decade. This comes at a time when residential resales are predicted by most to fluctuate between 3.5-3.8 million sales through the year 2000.

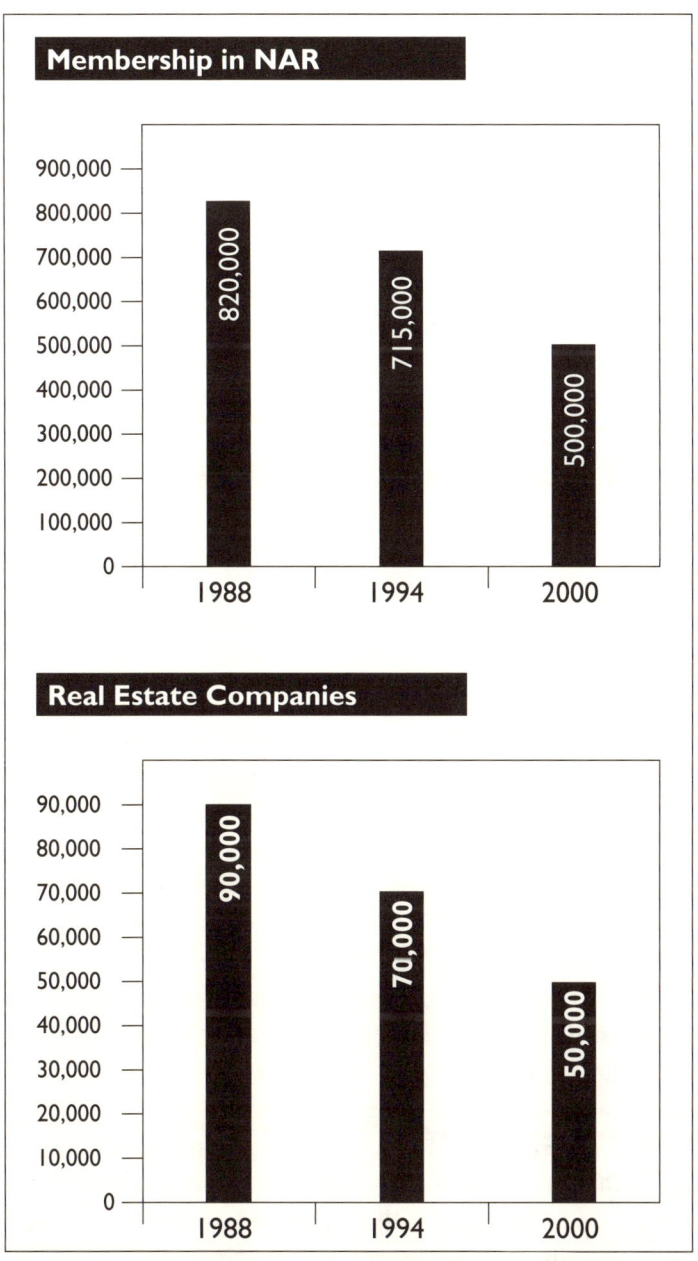

Fig. 1-A

All of which means that about the same amount of sales will be handled by a lot less people.

DRIVING FORCES

With sales relatively stable, what is driving some brokers out of the business? A variety of factors, including:

- *LACK OF PROFITABILITY:* The overall industry is strong in sales knowledge but weak in general business skills. Combine this with everyone wanting more for less and you have trouble. Agent splits have increased dramatically, while the commission charged consumers is trending downward. This margin decrease has been accelerated by the need to upgrade at all areas of the business and stay competitive with the current market.

- *TECHNOLOGY COSTS:* They have been steadily rising as computers, software, and high-tech office equipment have become indispensable tools. In many cases brokers have not yet replaced their paper systems, but have added computers without reducing costs.

- *COST OF SUPPORT SERVICES:* Increased competition in the marketplace means brokers must provide their associates better training, better advertising, better support in the office. And that can be costly.

- *AGENT SOPHISTICATION:* Agents themselves have come to expect all of the above — top-notch support services, high-tech equipment, and the like. The broker who is unable to provide all of this cannot attract the best agents.

- *LACK OF AGENT LOYALTY:* In the past, agents were more likely to stay put; today, they move around, depending on their individual needs. It can be difficult for a broker to build a strong team.

- *THE CHANGING CONSUMER:* Today's real estate consumer is, without a doubt, much smarter and more demanding than ever before. This consumer will not settle for second-rate service.

THE FALLOUT

All of these conditions and more are taking a toll on real estate practitioners who aren't well-trained, ethical and extremely professional. Meanwhile, the companies that are well-run, with well-trained, fully-supported agents and an emphasis on customer service, are thriving — sometimes in the same market as the struggling companies. It's a consumer-driven fallout, and one that will continue over the next few years.

And that raises an interesting question: What will become of those companies that continue to disappear from the real estate marketing landscape in the coming years? In many cases, they will be acquired by other aggressive, growing real estate companies. As the market consolidates, and many players continue to drop out, there will be more acquisition opportunities than ever before. And the companies that pursue and execute these acquisitions may well be at the forefront of the real estate business in the year 2000 and beyond. But only if they handle these acquisitions successfully... and that brings us to the purpose of this book.

THE ART OF ACQUISITION

The fact is, doing an acquisition well is both a science and an art form. It goes beyond the mere crunching of numbers into the subtleties of anticipating and shaping change. The process can be complex and even bewildering at times. But at the same time, there are common elements in almost all successful acquisitions, and there are clear and logical principles and steps that can help guide you through the minefield. (And it is a similar process regardless of whether you're acquiring 10 agents or 100.)

The goal of this book will be to lay out those guidelines in a manner that can be easily understood, and applied in the real world.

The interest in acquisitions is already fairly widespread in our business. A recent survey conducted among the top 100 real estate companies in U.S. found that 77 percent of them had been involved in one or more mergers or acquisitions; and 60 percent of them attributed a significant share of their growth to acquisitions. A drastic change to a similar survey done in 1985. (SEE CHART, FIG. 1-B). Clearly, the major players in real estate have identified acquisitions as a primary way to grow their companies in the years ahead.

But acquisition opportunities are not limited to only the giants of the business. You don't need to be huge: I've seen small-to-mid-size firms successfully acquire companies — sometimes acquiring a company many times larger than themselves. And you don't need tremendous amounts of capital, since many acquisitions in real estate today involve relatively small upfront cash payments. The bottom line is that as long as your company is progressive, well-run, ethical, and thoroughly professional, you probably have all the ingredients needed to be successful at an acquisition.

1980 - 1985

Top 100 Companies Involved
in a Merger or Aquisition

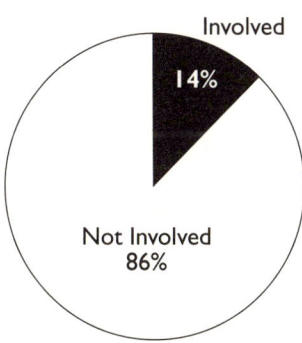

1990 - 1994

Top 100 Companies Involved
in a Merger or Aquisition

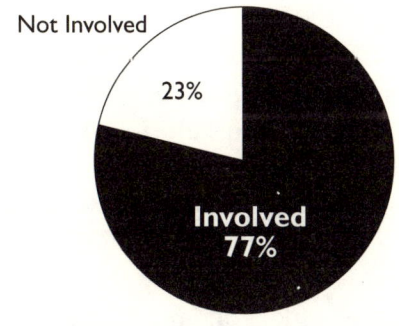

Fig. 1-B

Why Buy or Sell a Real Estate Company?

> ### TOP TEN REASONS TO ACQUIRE ANOTHER COMPANY
>
> 10. Increase visibility
> 9. Add a niche speciality to your company
> 8. Add outstanding facilities or services
> 7. Cost efficient use of your existing resources
> 6. Inject new life and energy into your company
> 5. Gain a presence in a prime location
> 4. Form a partnership with a talented owner/manager
> 3. Gain market share
> 2. Add a team of new agents
>
> *And the #1 reason:*
> *Become more profitable!*

Fig. 1-C

WHY BUY?

Assuming everything is going well in your own operation, why would you want to acquire another company? Why take on someone else's headaches? Actually, there are many reasons why an acquisition could make sense for your particular company (SEE CHECKLIST, FIG. 1-C).

An acquisition can provide a quick influx of listings and agents that can energize a company, and help it move to the next level. Naturally, you could bring in agents without an acquisition, via your own recruiting and training programs. But an acquisition is in many ways similar to the process of recruiting — only in group form. It enables you to bring in an entire team — already trained, already entrenched in the market, and ready to produce sales immediately. These agents will be the key to whether your acquisition is ultimately successful.

In addition to bringing in agents, an acquisition may be the fastest way to increase your market share and visibility in a given market — either in your current market or perhaps in a new market. Mario Polo, President of The Polo Group, an ERA company based in Tampa, Florida, found that when he merged with a comparably-sized brokerage in a nearby market a few years ago, the impact was startling: "As far as the community was concerned, I instantly had another 200 signs in the marketplace, which helped to attract customers and agents," he says. "Basically, by linking up with an existing company, we went from being a single market player to a multi-market player overnight."

Another potential benefit of an acquisition is that it can, in effect, fill the gaps in your operation — providing strength and support in specific areas where your company might be lacking. There are a variety of potential synergies that may exist between buyer and seller. For example, the company you acquire may be located on the other side of town — thereby providing you with complete market coverage. Or, it may specialize in a particular niche, such as waterfront properties; when you acquire the company, you acquire that niche. The company may have particular strength in a service area, such as property management or relocation, which can then be used to strengthen your own company. Or it may be adept at providing support to its own agents, through a strong marketing or training program; presumably, all of your agents stand to benefit from that after the acquisition.

EFFICIENT GROWTH

Finally, an acquisition can be the most cost-efficient way to expand and grow. As we've already noted, the consumer of the 90's is demanding that agents be better equipped — through training, technology, and support services — than ever before. But at the same time, profit margins have been squeezed dramatically in the 1990's as a result of increasing expenses for technology and marketing support, along with rising commission splits for agents.

In many cases, the only way for a broker to provide the necessary high-quality support to agents and service to the consumer — while still managing to turn a profit — is for that broker to operate as efficiently as possible. That service is often easier to provide and less costly in a medium or large operation. The fixed costs can be very similar for an office of 30 agents and one of 50 agents.

Similarly, a broker with 25 agents in one section of the city and another broker with 25 agents in a complementary market both have to pay for their own copiers, phone system, receptionist, and other facilities and services; but if you can combine those two offices through an acquisition or merger, overhead can be cut and more money can be dedicated to training, marketing, and support services.

Ken Ulsaker, owner of ERA Five Star Properties in Burke, Virginia, notes that when he acquired a competing real estate firm of a comparable size, it made the company more efficient in a number of ways. "It was easier to recruit, because we had much greater visibility. We combined training for all the offices, saved money on advertising efficiencies, saved money on printing because our volume increased, and were able to negotiate for better terms with bankers and vendors. As you get bigger, you just have more leverage in all your business relationships."

WHY SELL?

We've talked about reasons to buy another real estate company. But as you begin to explore the acquisition process, you should also consider the other side of this question: Why would someone be interested in selling their company to you? It's important to understand the rationale and the motivations of the seller — because that will enable you to develop the rapport that is crucial to a successful acquisition. So, why do people sell?

It could be any one of a number of reasons (SEE CHECKLIST, FIG. 1-D), including a case of burnout, loss of agents, personal reasons, partnership dispute, or legal problems. They may be just tired of the hassles: In many ways, running a real estate company is tougher and more demanding than ever today, and people may be tired of the various administrative and personnel challenges. They may be ready to pack it in and retire or start another career. Or they may just want to go back to selling real estate. Keep in mind that most of the people running real estate companies are agents who became owners; in the process, they were compelled to do a lot of

---

TOP TEN REASONS PEOPLE SELL A REAL ESTATE COMPANY

10. Burnout
9. Loss of agents
8. Personal or legal problems
7. Want access to better resources
6. Partnership dispute
5. Tired of managerial hassles
4. Retiring
3. Starting a new career
2. Going back to selling

And the #1 reason:
Not making money

Fig. 1-D

the things that agents typically don't like to do, such as paperwork and staff management. In effect, they get caught in the trap of being an owner and they find out — too late — that they actually liked and are better at real estate sales than real estate management.

THE MONEY ISSUE

So there may be a whole myriad of personal reasons pushing a broker toward selling, and you have to be aware of those. But in reality, about 90+ percent of the time you will find that the real driving force behind the decision to sell is money — or the lack of it. Because typically if someone's making enough money, they're not really thinking about retirement, or getting caught up in partnership disputes, or worrying about administrative hassles. So it's the financial problems that tend to bring out these other secondary issues. And the strange thing is, the first few times you talk to a seller, they'll keep talking about these secondary issues. But eventually as you talk further and really examine the company, you get to the heart of the matter — they're not getting back enough money for the time, energy, and resources invested.

This is an issue you, as a possible buyer, need to confront right away. Because if the real reason they're selling is that they're not profitable enough, then you need to be aware of how you're going to turn those problems around. And you're going to have to structure an acquisition so that when you take on their agents and their particular burdens, you're going to get different results... you're going to make money where they didn't.

THE WIN/WIN APPROACH

But at the same time, you must also figure out how to deal with some of the buyers' other concerns and needs — such as his own personal future, and that of his agents. Your objective should be to create a "win/win" outcome for both the buyer and the seller. Though people may buy and sell for different reasons, the two agendas can be brought together, so that everyone profits by the transaction.

Unfortunately, the "win/win" approach is not as common as it should be in real estate acquisition; far more prevalent is the tendency to view acquisitions as a form of competitive warfare (SEE CARTOON, FIG. 1-E). Buyers are more likely to think in terms of how inexpensively they can get a company, focusing only on the short term. It's true that you want to pay a fair amount — and less is always better from a monetary standpoint — but an acquisition can't be measured on a short-term basis; IT MUST BE LOOKED AT AFTER 1 TO 3 YEARS TO JUDGE WHETHER IT IS A SUCCESS.

And the key to achieving such long-term success is RETAINING THE AGENTS AND MAKING SURE THEY'RE PRODUCTIVE. That often becomes easier if the seller is on your side. This person may offer tremendous value as an agent, trainer, or manag-

Used with permission of Tribune Media Services

Fig. 1-E

er, and can help keep the operation running strong after the sale. That's why the "win/win" philosophy, which will be discussed throughout this book, is so important. It isn't just altruism — ultimately, it's a smart way and right way to do business, as we'll demonstrate.

THE SELLER'S PERSPECTIVE

It should be noted that this book is being presented primarily from the buyer's point of view — though if you're planning to sell your company, it can serve as a guide to help you understand the motivations and approaches of the various buyers you'll be negotiating with. I would, however, like to make a few specific points about selling (this information is also pertinent to buyers) before returning to the buyer's perspective.

To begin with, sellers should be aware that the only real value in a company is the gross revenue and net income that it can generate after a sale. Your company may be 35 years old, with a wonderful name and reputation, and you may have poured a tremendous amount of your life and resources into it through the years — but a buyer is far more concerned about the future than about history. The past is only of interest if it can demonstrate potentially more return. The buyer will pay based on the present and future value of your company, in terms of its profit potential.

Clearly, the best time to sell your company is when you're making a profit and on the upswing; the worst time is when you start losing market share and agents. So that means you should be thinking ahead: If you're considering selling 6 months or a year down the road, now is the time to begin to make your company as attractive as possible to a potential suitor. Some key things to keep in mind as you prepare for a sale:

1) Agent retention is critical;

2) Consolidate and eliminate your debt as much as possible;

3) Put your financial information into an easy-to-understand, accessible form;

4) Remember, once you've decided to sell, move quickly and make sure the company doesn't deteriorate. If you mentally check out of the business before you physically check out, the company can lose value during the short time you are negotiating with a buyer.

5) Try to do what's best long-term for staff members, agents, and yourself as the owner — and if you can cover all three of those interests in a positive way, that's when you should sell.

THE BUYER'S PERSPECTIVE

Returning to the buyer's perspective, the buyer, too, must have his/her house in order before pursuing an acquisition. If you don't have a solid reputation and you aren't perceived as having an ability to lead a company, it will be more difficult and costly to acquire another company. The reason is that sellers are usually looking out for their agents' future and their own — and they don't want to sell to someone who seems incapable of retaining agents and growing the company. And it's important for you, the buyer, to realize that an acquisition won't solve fundamental problems. YOU SHOULD HAVE A STRONG EXISTING INFRASTRUCTURE BEFORE EMBARKING ON AN ACQUISITION. If you're not good at training, or managing an office, or if you've had trouble retaining your own agents, those weaknesses will be compounded after an acquisition. An acquisition can bring a weak company down much more quickly.

Before pursuing an acquisition, it's a good idea to assess your own needs, and set some guidelines. Regarding needs, are you seeking increased production? Management assistance? Location? Capital? You might want to create a worksheet (SEE NEEDS WORKSHEET, FIG. 1-F, page 19), outlining your various needs. Also, it's important to set some basic guidelines at the outset, including:

- How much are you willing to pay?

- The minimum return you're willing to accept on your investment.

- The capital risks involved (can they be covered?)

- The amount of time you are willing to allocate for the acquisition and transition.

THE BOTTOM LINE: IMPROVED PROFIT

With all of the various considerations that must be weighed, there is one central point which should be emphasized above all else — and which will be stressed throughout this book. The objective in pursuing an acquisition is not just growth, but PROFITABLE growth. PROFITABILITY SHOULD ALWAYS BE THE CENTRAL MOTIVATING FORCE BEHIND ANY ACQUISITION.

That may seem like an obvious statement, but it's surprising how many people lose sight of the bottom line during an acquisition. They allow other interests and motivations to take precedence. For instance, people sometimes buy out a competitor for the sole purpose of putting that competitor out of business. And while it can be a sound strategy to eliminate competition, you have to be careful about veering into the dangerous territory of emotions. Sometimes people acquire other companies for the wrong reasons: There's a tremendous ego gratification involved in buying another company. If you get caught up in that, it can adversely affect your negotiating and reasoning skills. As much as possible, you must take the emotion out of this process and make it a pure business decision.

OTHER PITFALLS

There are many other pitfalls to be avoided in the acquisition process. In many ways, a real estate company acquisition is more complex and risky than other types of acquisitions, because of the nature of the real estate business. "With a real estate acquisition, you're not dealing so much with hard assets as with human resources," says Dr. Steve Franklin, an international business consultant with Global Access Learning, Inc. "That means you have to give more careful consideration to the quality of the people, and the culture of the company you're acquiring. If you buy the wrong company, you may end with a situation in which the agents may not perform well after the acquisition — or worse still, they may abandon you."

Indeed, a bad acquisition can actually end up harming the acquiring company: If you bring in agents that don't fit with your culture, they could end up driving out your existing agents or breeding unhappiness within your company. On the other hand, you may pay for things that you thought you were getting (such as furniture) and find that they're not part of the deal. Or, you may buy a company without the owner or a key employee staying — and later find out that that person was an indispensable part of the operation.

We'll be analyzing each of these potential problems in the pages ahead, as we sort through all of the pitfalls that are part of the acquisition process. If you can avoid the pitfalls, you can arrive at what should be your ultimate goal: profitable growth. In the final analysis, the primary — and really the only — reason for embarking on an acquisition should be to make more money. And you must consider the profit picture before — not after — the acquisition. It's surprising how many brokers will communicate by their actions: "I'm going to go out and acquire an additional 50 agents — and then I'll figure out how to make money with those agents." When you just add agents for the sake of adding, you may end up buying agents, listings, market share... and less or no profit.

That's been proven many times in the past by some of the larger national companies, whose acquisition binges in the real estate business weren't always profitable. So one of the key things we're going to explore in the coming chapters is that fine line between acquiring for ego or market share, as opposed to acquiring for purposes of making more money. To insure the success of your acquisition, always focus on the latter.

Broker Needs Analysis
WORKSHEET

1. Company strengths:

2. Company challenges:

3. Broker strengths:

4. Competitive advantages:

5. Competitive future needs:

6. Where would I like the company and myself to be in 1 year?

Fig. 1-F

7. Where would I like the company and myself to be in three years?

8. How can I best get there?

9. I am willing to devote _____ % of time and $_____ to an acquisition program.

10. I would consider this year a success if...?

11. I would consider the acquisition program a success if...?

12. The most important element of my company I would want to retain under any circumstances...?

13. The major area of my company that an acquisition would help is...?

Fig. 1-F

CHAPTER TWO

The Basics

If you're going to expand by joining forces with another company, the first thing you must decide is whether to MERGE with that company or ACQUIRE it. Though the terms "merger" and "acquisition" are often used interchangeably, there are important differences.

Interestingly, you'll hear many people in real estate use the term "merger" to describe what is essentially an acquisition. The reason is that "merger" is a kinder, gentler term which suggests a spirit of cooperation between the two parties involved; "acquisition," to some, may connote that one party is "taking over" the other. But the truth of the matter is that an acquisition can — and should — be as friendly and cooperative as a merger. The only real difference is that in an acquisition, ownership of the combined companies is retained by one party (the buyer) rather than being divided among the two parties.

WHAT IS A MERGER?

A merger of two corporations typically involves the transfer of stock to a new partner or partners. Along with that transfer of ownership there is, typically, a transfer of some management control, too. GENERALLY SPEAKING, WITH A MERGER YOU ARE TAKING ON A FULL OR LIMITED PARTNER — WHO IS LIKELY TO BECOME PART OF THE DECISION-MAKING PROCESS AT THE NEW COMPANY. Obviously, in such a situation, an owner is giving up some level of control over the business.

Why would you choose to take this route? It could be that you desire a partnership, for a number of reasons (SEE CHECKLIST, FIG. 2-A). For example, a broker may be in need of management help and support. That broker may be strong in one management aspect — say, sales management — but weak in another area, such as administrative leadership. Or the broker may find that he/she likes to "work in the field" with the agents, as opposed to sticking around the office to oversee marketing and other functions.

A partner who has complementary strengths may be that missing link needed to grow your company and make it more well-rounded. And that partner can relieve some of the decision-making burdens — providing a second voice and perspective, to help make the tough choices. In such a scenario, if you can find a truly compatible partner, then a merger can be an outstanding opportunity. There are many, many successful partnerships around the country — and typically they involve partners who work well together, share a common vision, and also complement each other's skills.

RAISING CAPITAL

There may also be financial reasons behind choosing to do a merger. If, for example, your profits have plateaued and you need

> ### Pros and Cons of a Merger
>
> *Pros:*
> Gain power
> Gain competencies
> Raise capital
>
> *Cons:*
> Give up ownership
> Give up control
> Must answer to partner

Fig. 2-A

to raise capital for continued growth and investment, a merger may make sense. In effect, a merger allows you to trade off a certain amount of ownership for an infusion of resources — agents, listings, facilities, cash flow, and perhaps expertise — that can help "jump-start" your company and take it to the next level. Of course, you could also raise capital by bringing in an investor, but with a merger partner, you get more than just capital; you get agents, listings, and other assets that are already in place and ready to produce.

It's not uncommon to find that mergers occur between two companies of similar size and stature; if both companies are on a par with each other, for example, neither one may feel comfortable selling to the other. Tommy McIntosh, a co-owner of ERA Trend Realty in Gainesville, Fl., had talked for several years about acquiring a competing firm of equal size. The problem was that the other firm was interested in acquiring his company. "We couldn't work out an acquisition, and meanwhile the dominant company in the market was becoming more dominant," he says. "So we decided to join forces as equals — and that enabled us to reach critical mass and really challenge the market leader." As a general rule, if a company is up-and-coming and has a strong management, it may make more sense to view that company as a possible merger partner; conversely, if the company and its management seem to be winding down, they may be more of an acquisition candidate.

The Basics

GIVING UP CONTROL

But keep in mind that when you give up ownership by way of a merger, you may be instantly losing something that is very important to you — the ability to control your own destiny. "The issue of control is the central question when deciding between a merger and an acquisition," says acquisitions expert Dr. Steve Franklin, of Global Access Learning. As Franklin notes, a merger may necessitate that you now collaborate and negotiate with your new partner on everything from internal policy matters (such as commission splits) to the sharing of expenses and even the name of the company.

This can be a problem for many real estate brokers, who are used to being entrepreneurs and running their own show. Chances are, they've spent years growing a team and shaping a culture that reflects their own philosophy. They also may enjoy certain freedoms of ownership; since the real estate business often tends to combine work and personal life, some brokers may be used to going on trips and paying for it out of the company, or paying for their car, or paying a spouse's salary, all out of the company budget. When you take on a partner, be prepared to answer for all of that — everything should be and must be accounted for.

Those who do opt for a merger partnership should be very careful about who they choose as a partner. If there's any potential for conflict between partners, it's likely to be exacerbated in a post-merger environment. Because you don't really get a chance to learn and grow with your new partner — all of a sudden you're there in the midst of a good-sized company, having to make major decisions together. It's important to do a lot of research upfront as to what the operating plan and business plan and responsibilities will be to avoid misunderstandings and conflicts. But beyond these operational and monetary issues, you should have a sense of how the personalities and cultures of the partners will mix. So it's a good idea to have in-depth pre-merger meetings and discussions, in which everything is spelled out — e.g., "If X happens, then we'll do this, and if Y happens, we'll do that." It is always suggested to have an effective buy-sell agreement agreed to and signed prior to the merger. That's part of establishing a mutual vision, commitment, and an effective partnership upfront.

Given these concerns, it's not surprising that most owners of real estate companies would prefer to have lieutenants rather than partners — which is why acquisitions tend to be the preferred strategy for many brokers. (SEE CHECKLIST, FIG. 2-B).

In the subsequent chapters, we'll be talking primarily about acquisitions, rather than mergers. But keep this in mind: IT'S NOT A BAD IDEA TO USE THE TERM "MERGER" AS MUCH AS POSSIBLE, EVEN IF WHAT'S TRANSPIRING IS TECHNICALLY AN ACQUISITION. Because if you're acquiring a company that has a good reputation, the egos of the broker and his agents are involved.

That broker has put his/her life and heart into building up the company, and doesn't want to appear to have failed or "sold out." They'd rather be able to go to their country club and say, "I merged with ABC Realty, and we're now the number 1 company in town — isn't that great?" It also may make it easier for the broker who's being acquired to break the news to his/her own agents. It's so much more positive for them to say, "We've merged with ABC

PROS AND CONS OF AN ACQUISITION

Pros:	*Cons:*
Increase size and market share	Must pay for company
Maintain full control	Possible defections
Economics of scale created	Financial uncertainty
Jump start to everything	Larger "everything" immediately

Fig. 2-B

Realty and now we're able to accelerate our growth plans and build an exciting new company together — and it's going to be a tremendous opportunity for all of us." Contrast that to telling the staff or community, "I'm tired of the business, so I decided to sell out." It's a totally different attitude.

THE TWO TYPES OF ACQUISITIONS

Assuming you want to proceed with an acquisition rather than a merger, you'll most likely choose between two different types of acquisitions:

- The first kind involves the assumption of an existing operation; we'll refer to this as a "MOVE-IN." In this type of acquisition, you would keep the seller's offices open, retain the agents, keep the company's basic structure, and maintain an ongoing relationship with the seller. In effect, you would just move in and change signs.

- The second type of acquisition is known as a "FOLD-IN." In a fold-in, you would close down a seller's existing operation and acquire the agents. You would then integrate those agents seamlessly into your own company. (SEE CHART ON 2 TYPES OF ACQUISITIONS, FIG. 2-C.) A multi-office acquisition could obviously involve a combination of the two types.

BENEFITS OF A MOVE-IN

There are a couple of reasons why it might make sense to maintain the existing operation of another company. Location is probably the most important factor: If the company you're acquiring has a prime location, or they're located in a market you want to develop, it might make sense to just keep the operation in place. You might also be drawn to this type of acquisition if the seller has an outstanding facility — say, a modern, high-tech building, with great signage and visibility in the marketplace.

The problem, however, is that moving in and changing signs may not be all that's required to be successful in that location. If the company is selling to you because they're not making money (which is likely), then you'll need a strong plan for rejuvenating that operation — perhaps by integrating some of your original agents into the acquired office, or by bringing new management on board at that location. But remember that even if your company has

THE TWO TYPES OF ACQUISITIONS

Type	*How it Works*	*Reasons for doing it*
Move-In	Keep office open	Desire a stronger presence in their primary market; Good location; good facility; less disruptive to acquired agents
Fold-in	Close office; Bring acquired agents into your office	Consolidation of services; cost efficient; greater control integrating two cultures

Fig. 2-C

The Basics

a strong, success-oriented culture, it may be difficult to instill that culture into a remote office. After the acquisition, they may continue to run for a long time by doing things the way they're used to doing them. And that can quickly degenerate in an "us-versus-them" situation (as with any company branch office that is not considered "the main office").

Beyond that, the process of assuming existing operations carries greater financial risk (SEE "MOVE-IN" CASE STUDY, ADDENDUM A, PAGE 165). You will probably have to do many of the same things you're doing with your own company to recruit and retain existing agents — and since the offices are separate, that may necessitate duplication of services. When you assume existing operations, there's less opportunity to consolidate and save money on overhead. On the contrary, you may find overhead costs soaring as you try to get the "new office" up and running at full speed.

THE TREND TOWARD FOLD-INS

That's why fold-ins are becoming increasingly common as more and more companies open large regional offices. The fold-in approach plays into the industrywide trend of consolidation: You're going to maximize profitability because you'll have agents coming into an existing fixed-expense program — which should result in an exponential increase in your bottom line. (SEE "FOLD-IN" CASE STUDY, ADDENDUM B, PAGE 171).

There are also other reasons to opt for a fold-in. Typically, you can have much better control over the integration of the two cultures. And you can generate new enthusiasm at your own company, with an influx of new agents into the office. As those new agents come into your company, you can gradually begin to pick and choose the best and eventually (as quickly as possible) let go of the rest.

It should be noted that a fold-in can sometimes be a more complicated and demanding acquisition. The negotiation process may be more complex because the seller may have a facility and equipment and other assets that are being left behind — and you may have to assist in figuring out what to do about that. (For instance, the seller might be unable to sell these fixed assets, and may want you to take them on as part of the transaction; we'll talk about how you can deal with this scenario in later chapters).

A fold-in also may be disruptive to the agents that you're acquiring: If your facility is not comparable and doesn't offer the same services, or if its location is in a different market or on the fringe of the current office, the seller's agents might begin to look elsewhere instead of making a move to a location they feel is inconvenient to the market they serve.

DON'T BE SCARED OFF

But there are ways to resolve these potential conflicts, as you'll see. In general, acquisitions are not as difficult or costly as you might think. Don't let the term scare you. While some people assume that acquisitions can only be understood by lawyers or financial experts, that's not the case. You may need some help along the way — i.e., some legal advice when drawing up a contract or financial advice when reviewing someone's books. And it's probably a good idea to seek out another broker who's done an acquisition for some tips. But most of the process can be done face-to-face between the buyer and seller, without anyone else involved.

And don't think that you are unable to do an acquisition because of limited resources, either. In the early days of real estate acquisitions, most of the purchase price was paid upfront; buyers quickly learned that sellers could and would walk across the street and open another company, and then whisk away agents and customers. With that in mind, current purchases of real estate firms tend to be based on a deferred payout structure that runs from one year to three years, with the risk shared by the buyer and seller. Generally, you don't need a tremendous amount of cash up front to do an acquisition.

BASIC GUIDELINES

As I said earlier, the acquisition process is an art as well as a science — and in fact, it's more art than science. When you try to place a value on a company using some of the formulas that we'll show you, you will probably find that there's no consistent consensus on what company A is worth — it depends on the market, who's buying, and the terms of the transaction. There are many variables, and a lot of room for flexibility.

But at the same time, there ARE specific steps and guidelines you can follow (just as when you recruit individual agents — each agent is different, but the successful brokers tend to follow a process). In the many acquisitions I've been involved with, I've found that there is a basic 10-step process that seems to apply to almost any acquisition. The steps are as follows:

1) Identify quality candidates.

2) Establish contact with those candidates, by calling them, meeting with them, and making a presentation.

3) Build a relationship and analyze the needs of that candidate.

4) Gather information on the company.

5) Evaluate that company — both financially and in terms of potential fit with your own company.

6) Create a letter of intent and a new company vision.

7) Develop a transition plan.

8) Go to contract and close the deal.

9) Integrate the two companies, with particular emphasis on retaining agents.

10) Evaluate your results, return to step one and begin anew with your next acquisition.

In the following chapters, we'll break down each of these steps. Remember, this process may take one month or it may take a year or two years (we've found that most true acquisitions happen in a period of less than three months, once the talks become serious). But however long it takes, you almost always have to go through these steps without skipping any of them. These steps will guide you through the process in a logical and orderly fashion, and help you arrive at your ultimate goal — a successful and profitable acquisition.

CHAPTER THREE

Getting Started: Identifying Candidates

Once you've determined that an acquisition fits with your overall business strategy, the first step is to identify some companies that you might be interested in acquiring. Sounds simple enough — but in fact you may find that there are many, many potential candidates worthy of at least some consideration. People embarking on an acquisition often make the mistake of ruling out potential candidates based on faulty assumptions. Don't assume, for example, that a company with a strong track record would be unwilling to sell or unaffordable. If you rule out candidates in this manner, you may miss out on a great opportunity. You should consider almost EVERYONE to be a potential candidate.

As we discussed in Chapter 1, the primary reason that companies sell can often be traced to a failure to make money. You may find that a smaller firm in your market with just a few agents is having a hard time keeping pace with larger competitors. But on the other hand, the same kinds of financial difficulties are often faced by the mid-sized companies, too; in many cases, their growth may have stalled at the middle range, keeping them from achieving critical mass from a monetary standpoint.

BIGGER COMPANIES MAY BE CANDIDATES

Even a larger company can be viewed as a candidate. Don't assume that you can only acquire a company that is smaller than your own. There have been cases of companies acquiring someone twice their size, with twice as many agents. Chet Hogan, owner of ERA Associate Realty of Indian River, based in Vero Beach, Fla., acquired a firm with 35 agents — though his firm at the time had just 16 agents. Similarly, Ken Ulsaker, owner of ERA Five Star Properties in Burke, Va., acquired a company with six offices — though his firm only had three offices at the time. And Ulsaker says that despite the size of the company he acquired, it wasn't a costly acquisition: "We didn't have to pay much money upfront," he says. Part of the reason Ulsaker was able to acquire the company was that it was having difficulties, and the owner was anxious to sell. A large company may also consider selling a branch office or two that haven't done well.

But this doesn't necessarily mean that a candidate must be in deep financial trouble before they'll be willing to sell to you. A company may actually be doing well, but the owner may be anxious for a change anyway — particularly if there's a personal problem or disruption in that person's life, or if they've simply decided to give up the management headaches and go back to selling. Obviously, the advantage of acquiring a company that is doing well financially is that you know there's great potential for that operation to continue to be profitable for you, without requiring a major overhaul.

On the other hand, you might find that the best opportunities, pricewise, can be found among companies that are struggling — but which have the potential to do better under your leadership. Remember that a struggling company can represent an opportunity, provided you have the ability to change and improve that company. It may be that there's nothing wrong with the agents — except that they lack sufficient leadership and support under the current owner.

Gloria Frazier, President of American Realty of Northwest Florida, acquired one company that was "about to go under," she says, because the firm was undercapitalized and lacked strong management. After the acquisition, Frazier provided the training and support services that had been so needed by those agents — and she saw their sales performance improve dramatically the next year. So it's important not to rule out marginal players because of their size or past sales performance; as long as a company is ethically sound, they should be considered a potential candidate.

FINDING A NICHE

You may choose to look for candidates within a PARTICULAR NICHE, such as property management, if your goal is to strengthen a specific aspect of your overall company. There are any number of potential compatible niche markets, such as:

1) Luxury homes

2) Acreage

3) Commercial/ Investment

4) Condos

5) Waterfront properties

6) Property Management

7) Resort Properties

8) Development

9) International

10) Ethnic markets

As you can see, there are many niche possibilities that you can look for in other companies. Also, as you seek out candidates, remember that you needn't necessarily acquire an entire company: THERE'S ALSO THE OPTION OF ACQUIRING A COMPANY-WITHIN-A-COMPANY. We're seeing more cases now in which a mega-producing lead agent — who may have six or seven agents working for him or her — is identified as an acquisition prospect. Rather than bringing in the whole company, you would simply bring this group into your company in a fold-in arrangement.

ETHICALLY SOUND CANDIDATES

Is there anyone who shouldn't be considered a candidate? Probably the only companies that you should automatically steer clear of would be those that are not ethically sound. The need for professionalism is so critical in today's real estate marketplace, that if a company has a bad reputation —- and if that reputation is well-founded based on behavior — then such an alliance could tarnish your whole company's image. So, you should be on the lookout for companies that don't deliver good customer service or whose agents promise things to sellers and don't back it up. Even if such a company were available to you for free, it probably wouldn't be in your best interests to acquire them.

But keep this in mind: Occasionally, agents with a struggling company get an unfair rap. Try to be certain that the reputation you're hearing about a company's agents is legitimate. To distinguish between the perceived reputation and the legitimate one, investigate a little bit by talking to people who've actually done business with the agents. Remember that if the agents are fundamentally sound, you don't have to worry so much about the old company's reputation — after all, those agents will be changing their corporate identity and coming into your company, enabling them to leave that past reputation behind.

As you begin to consider candidates, remember that there's no harm in inquiring about whether companies are interested in selling — as long as you handle your inquiries properly (in Chapter 5, we'll discuss ways to approach candidates). At the very least, you'll probably find that most people are curious about why you're interested in their company. We often go into markets and ask if companies are interested in selling, and we find that almost 100 percent of them will talk with us just out of curiosity.

BEGINNING THE SEARCH

So at this point you've determined that there are potential sellers all around you — but how do you let those people know that you're a potential buyer? If you are serious about finding the best acquisition candidate, you must establish an identity among these potential candidates; it must be clear to them that your company is interested in acquisitions. If you don't achieve such visibility, you'll lose out to other companies that are known to specialize in acquisitions. Candidates will naturally gravitate toward whomever's most known, active, and visible in the acquisitions market.

To establish a presence as an aggressive, acquisition-minded company, you begin to go through a process that is very similar to an agent beginning to service a particular market area. It's a matter of getting the word out to the market all around you in a variety of ways; in effect, you're planting seeds everywhere, which may eventually bear fruit with an acquisition. You may initially be reaching out to people who aren't actively looking to sell —

because perhaps they never realized that selling was a viable option for them. As you begin to gradually work these candidates over a period of time — maybe a month or a year or more — eventually they may become more and more intrigued with the idea of selling, particularly as they begin to encounter problems or frustrations in their business.

There are a number of ways to get your message out there to the community, including:

• Advertising

• Direct Mail

• Word-of-Mouth

Beginning with ADVERTISING, a classified ad in a local newspaper or magazine or any real estate publication can be very effective. (SEE FIG. 3-A, SAMPLE CLASSIFIED AD). I know of a company that has published a classified ad in their little real estate board newsletter for the last five years: It just says, "If you're interested in selling your real estate company, please give us a call." They run that every month, and they've acquired a dozen small companies in their market.

Typically, advertising will solicit a response (usually smaller companies) with the promise of confidentiality; the ad may say something like, "Growing real estate company interested in expanding in the Oakland area; please apply confidentially." But keep in mind that if you use the word "confidential," you'd better abide by that — or you'll lose all credibility with the other brokers in that community. The worst thing you can do is start telling people in the market, "I almost acquired Jones Realty down the street, but I decided the company wasn't good enough." That will raise concerns — and rightfully so — about what you're telling competitors about each other.

> ESTABLISHED RESIDENTIAL REAL ESTATE COMPANY seeks to expand operations in the Greater Atlanta market by buying or merging with established companies. Interested companies (principles only) please send pertinent information (last 2 years P&L, listing inventory, etc.) to CEO, P.O. Box 144, Atlanta, GA 30084. All data will be held in complete confidentiality.

Sample Classified Ad   Fig. 3-A

DIRECT MAIL

Perhaps even more effective than advertising is DIRECT MAIL — which may be one of your best tools in getting word out to the market that you're serious about acquisitions. (SEE FIG. 3-B, SAMPLE DIRECT MAIL PIECE). Again, this can be just a simple, straightforward message: For example, if you're doing a mailing to your board, you might tell members, "We enjoyed cooperating with your company over the last year, and if you're ever interested in doing something different with your company or real estate career, give me a call."

But to be truly effective, your direct mail must be consistent; monthly or every other month, you must get that acquisition reminder in front of people (in much the same way you would consistently direct-mail a potential recruit). Because when you first present the possibility of selling to a broker, they're generally going to reject the idea. But as times get tougher, they're increasingly aware of this other option you keep suggesting to them... and then your direct mail just might show up the day they're feeling most frustrated. And that's when they'll pick up the phone and give you a call.

Dear _____,

The real estate business as you know offers constantly changing opportunities and challenges. Our company has been very fortunate to experience many successes recently. We are interested in continuing our growth through possible mergers with professional companies and people like yourself.

I want to personally invite you to discuss the future of real estate in our market. Please call me for a completely confidential conversation on the possibility of two great companies merging.

At the very least, we can explore the opportunities in today's real estate market.

Let's have breakfast or lunch at your earliest convenience. Please call me at _____.

Sincerely,

Fig. 3-B

Sample Direct Mail Piece

WORD-OF-MOUTH

Don't underestimate the power of WORD-OF-MOUTH. By talking to your own agents, you can find out a lot of things you might not know about other companies in the market. You should also talk to:

• People at mortgage companies

• Insurance companies

• Attorneys

• Sign installers and quick-print companies

• Market magazines

These kinds of people tend to know when a particular company may be in trouble or looking for a change. And board secretaries and executives happen to be a great source of information about who's looking to sell a company.

Also, your agents can get involved in spreading the word throughout the market that your company is looking to buy. This is something the agents can be proud of — it makes them feel good to say, "Our company's growing and we're looking to add another company."

MLS REPORTS

Undoubtedly, as you search for candidates you'll find yourself relying extensively on MLS Reports. They are particularly useful when it comes to spotting trends. (SEE GRAPH FROM MLS

REPORT, FIG. 3-C). Is a company going up or down? If it's moving primarily downward, the company may be facing some stiff challenges — which could present opportunities for you to help them. If they're doing well, and they're located in a complementary market, they might be the first candidates to look at in terms of branching out — because it's easier to assume an existing operation if that operation is sound.

Through most multiple listing services, you can determine average sales price and amount of inventory your competitors are taking on a monthly basis, how much of that actually sells, and the market that they serve from a listing and sales standpoint. You can even look at performance of individual agents — so that you can see if one or two agents are responsible for a lot of the sales. Even if you have to hire a temporary assistant to hand count the activity, this information is extremely valuable in helping you begin to sift through the candidates and come up with a target list.

TRACKING CANDIDATES

As you get down to a suggested target list of 6 or 7 candidates, it's not a bad idea to track your target candidates over a period of time. First, go back over the last six months and look at the trends for each of those companies over that period. You also want to track them on a month-by-month basis within that period — to see if they've been consistent in terms of sales price, listing price, inventory, or if agents have been coming or going. That way, when it comes time for your first meeting (which we'll get to in the next chapter), you can say, "Well, I see you've gone up by X percent in the last six months," or "I see that your sales dipped a little in September."

You may also want to begin to investigate the reputations of the companies you're interested in. You can talk to your own agents,

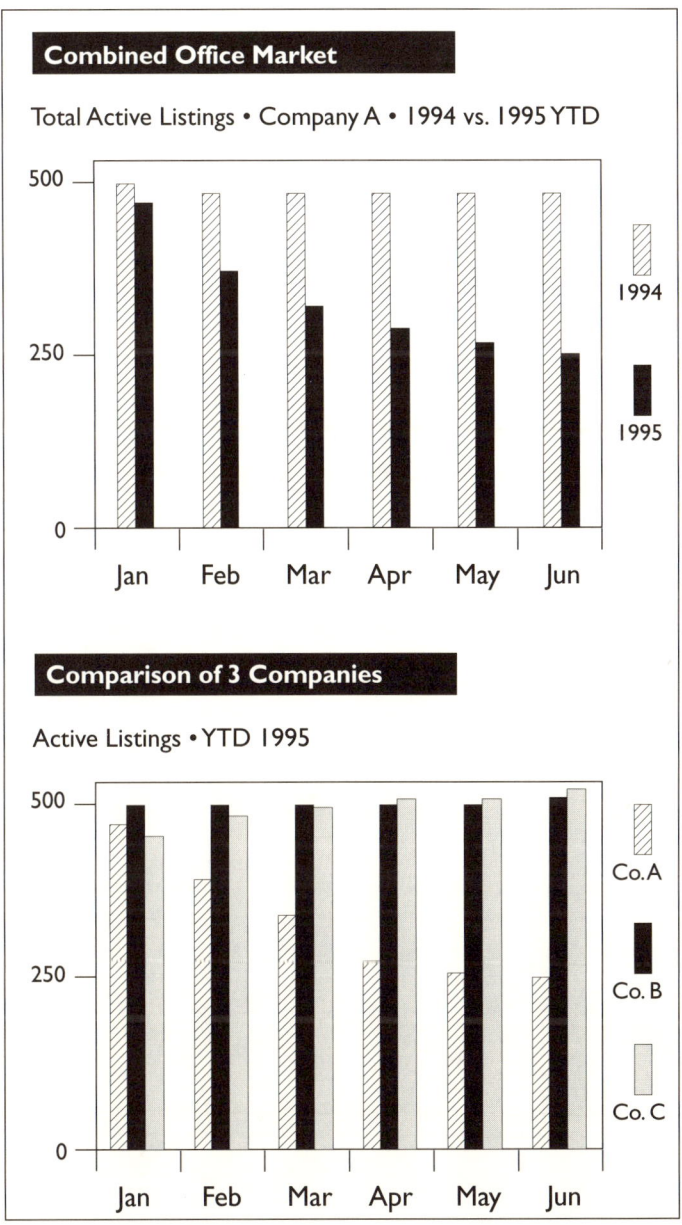

Fig. 3-C

Getting Started: Identifying Candidates

who may be able to tell you about co-op experiences with these companies' agents. Also, the mortgage companies, title companies, and attorneys in town may have worked with them (remember to be cautious when making inquiries; you want to be able to approach the candidates confidentially). Try to find out what these people are like to work with. Inquire about how strong the management is. You can even call the agents at your target companies as part of a recruiting effort, and try to find out a little bit about how well the company is run.

Now admittedly, all of this involves a lot of work — and you may not ever acquire the company in question. But a lot of the information you're gathering is valuable in any case; in the 90's, you really need to know what your competitors' strengths and weaknesses are, and that's what you're evaluating here. As you learn more about other companies in your marketplace, you may also learn valuable lessons about your own company. And the entire process will prepare you for the next big stage — when you actually begin to call upon candidates and set the acquisition in motion.

CHAPTER FOUR

Approaching a Candidate

Once you've compiled a list of potential candidates for an acquisition, you arrive at what just might be the most difficult part of the acquisition process — approaching those candidates.

Breaking the ice is never easy, and that's probably the main reason why so many would-be acquisitors put off making that first phone call to a candidate. Instead, they'll spend weeks analyzing data on a company. And then they'll put that analysis aside and say, "I'll get back to this acquisition stuff later." When they do get back to it, they start all over again with more analysis. Before you know it, six months have gone by and they're still at the stage of doing basic research. By that time, there's a good chance they'll grow tired of the whole thing and just drop it.

Analysis is necessary, of course, but remember — THE ACQUISITION PROCESS DOESN'T REALLY GET STARTED UNTIL YOU MAKE THAT FIRST CALL. And if you delay in making that call, you stand to miss out on great opportunities.

At the same time, it's important not to rush things as you get to this stage. Starting an acquisition is exciting, but if you're too anxious or aggressive in your initial approach to a candidate, you can easily scare them off. That's why your initial conversations with a candidate shouldn't include words like "takeover," or "closedown," or anything along those lines. You have to build slowly. And you should begin by merely suggesting that you would like to get together to talk about the real estate business and about possible opportunities to work together.

FINDING THE RIGHT APPROACH

As you establish contact with a candidate, the approach and the tone that you adopt will set the stage for future conversations. We will examine a number of different approaches, and see how they are used in some sample calls to candidates. As you'll see, there are instances in which the caller may choose a more "direct" approach — which might be appropriate in a situation in which you need to move ahead quickly (such as with a struggling company). Or you may opt for more of a "soft sell" when dealing with a more successful candidate, who may not have previously considered selling their company. (SEE CHART ON HARD & SOFT SELL, FIG. 4-A).

HARD SELL VS. SOFT SELL

Hard Sell:

"We're interested in expanding"
"Have you ever thought about selling your company"

Soft Sell:

"Let's have lunch"
"Where are you headed with your company and real estate"

Fig. 4-A

SAMPLE FIRST CALLS

Everyone has their own particular conversational style, and it's best to be as natural as possible when first talking to a candidate. If you follow a rehearsed script too closely, the call may end up sounding like a canned pitch that you've tried on a dozen other brokers. Still, it can be useful to look at the following "first call" scripts, provided courtesy of Mark Masters, president of ERA Prestige Homes in Medford, Oregon. Masters has completed many successful acquisitions, most of which got started with a phone conversation that went something like this:

"Hi Bill, this is Mark Masters over at ERA Prestige Homes... Do you have a minute?... I keep on hearing from my agents about what a good company you have and how my people enjoy working with your people, so I thought to myself — wouldn't it be nice if we could get together for lunch sometime and maybe figure a few different ways our companies could work even closer together? What do you think?"

Masters says he sometimes uses a couple of variations on this particular dialogue. Here's one, in which Masters suggests working together against a "common enemy" in the market:

"Hi Bill, this is Mark Masters over at ERA Prestige Homes... Do you have a minute to talk?... Bill, I've been watching ABC Realty's hold on the east side of town strengthen every year since 1989 — I can't seem to break in. The reason I'm calling is that I've got a few ideas on how to break their grip by double-teaming with another company, and I would like to have somebody to bounce those ideas off. I also would like to throw some ideas at you on something that might be mutually beneficial to both of us. Would you have a lunch hour free this week?"

Finally, Masters has what he calls the "hard sell" approach:

"Hi Bill, this is Mark Masters over at ERA Prestige Homes... You got a minute? ... Bill, we are going to be expanding into the Medford area soon, and we are currently looking for a partner that

Approaching a Candidate   47

we can add our strengths to in order to dominate that market. In our search, you and your company are one of the most respected in that market. The reason I am calling is this: If I could show you a way that by working with us, I can guarantee you the same profit you've been making so far — without taking any risk or having to worry about any bills — and also get 50 percent or more of your time back to build your company or just relax, do you think that would be worth hearing about?"

Notice that none of these conversations are overly specific. The sole purpose of the call is to set up a casual meeting, over breakfast or lunch, to talk about the real estate market. Generally, you will not get turned down when you make such a simple request. In fact, most real estate people love to talk about the business, and learn a little more about the competition.

If someone isn't willing to take the time to meet with you for breakfast or lunch, that could be a bad sign. It may be an indication that this particular broker is not open-minded or interested in what's happening outside his/her business, or that he/she simply doesn't trust anybody. In that case, the person may not be an ideal candidate; it would be difficult to build a relationship with someone like that.

PERSISTENCE PAYS OFF

On the other hand, don't give up too soon. A lot of people may be taken aback when you first call; you're catching them off guard, and they're not sure what you're really up to, and that could be the reason for their trepidation. Masters says that if he encounters resistance to his initial suggestion for a meeting, he adds this: "Let me ask you: Can you see any disadvantage in just hearing what I have to say?" Indeed, the candidate can only benefit from such a meeting, which should be pointed out. You might say: "Look, at the very least, you'll know a little bit more about my company and I'll know a little bit more about yours, and maybe we can do more business together in the future."

If you can't convince someone to meet with you, then at that point, you should just be friendly and courteous and say: "Well, maybe we can get together in a couple of months." And then put it on your calendar to call six or eight weeks later. Because during those two months, a lot of changes can and do happen. In my dealings with acquisition candidates, I've seen people continue to say no for two years — then suddenly you call them and they're ready to talk. It's all a matter of timing.

Some brokers prefer to avoid cold-calling candidates; they would rather initiate the conversation in a more casual circumstance. For example, Gloria Frazier says she tries to arrange to be in the same room with a candidate, at which point she begins a conversation that gradually introduces the possibility of working together. "I'd prefer not to call people on the phone because it makes it seem like I'm really going after them, and that could make the price go up," Frazier says. "So instead, I'll try to get myself seated next to that broker at a board lunch. Also, my company hosts lunches and we invite other brokers in the community. I'd rather begin talking to someone more casually, and then at some point suggest getting together for a meeting to talk more about working together."

THE FIRST MEETING

Whether it's achieved through a cold-call, direct mail, or through a bit of cocktail party maneuvering, the end result of your initial contact should be to have a meeting set up. Who should be at that first meeting? It depends. If there are a couple of partners involved at the other company, you might start out talking to one and then with the other; I have found it is usually easier to share your vision with one person at a time. With regard to spouses, it's preferable to just get the principal there without the spouse on the first meeting or two — though you will want to involve the spouse before too long, as we'll discuss later.

In setting up that first meeting, you will need to:

- Determine the participants

- Choose a neutral site

- Prepare a letter of confidentiality

- Do some homework on the candidate's company

The meeting should be held in a neutral site — a restaurant is a good choice — and it's probably a good idea to hold the meeting somewhere outside the market area. If you meet in the middle of town, there's a greater chance that someone might see the two of you talking, and start rumors. If somebody comes up to the seller later on and says, "I saw you talking to John, are you two thinking of merging?" — that could rattle the seller and cause him to break off talks.

CONFIDENTIALITY IS CRITICAL

From the buyer's standpoint, you should do everything possible to prevent such a thing from happening. At some point, you and the seller should both sign a letter of confidentiality (SEE SAMPLE 4-B), which basically says that all information exchanged in the ensuing conversations will be kept in confidence. The timing for this may be the first or second meeting, usually after both agree to explore possibilities further through additional discussions. In addition, you should make sure that everyone at your own company who may know about these conversations — such as your bookkeeper, or perhaps your secretary who's setting up the meetings or taking the calls — also understands the importance of maintaining absolute confidentiality during an acquisition. This is a critical matter and your employees should know that; if information leaks, it can cause the potential loss of agents for the seller. It also could kill the potential transaction, and it might damage any future attempts to talk to other brokers in the community, because they'll be worried that you can't maintain a confidential trust.

Prior to the meeting, do some homework so that you will be able to talk intelligently about the company. You should know the company's market position, how they've been doing lately in terms of listings and sales, a little bit about their people, perhaps something about their advertising that you may have noticed in the last month or two. You want to let the seller know that this is more than just a casual meeting, and that you have taken a genuine interest in their company. That is flattering to them, and it also tells them that you really do have your finger on the pulse of the marketplace. You might start off the meeting by telling the candidate about yourself — where your company has been and where it's going, and what are the challenges and opportunities you face (be careful, however, not to brag or boast about your company's accomplishments). This may coax the seller to begin to talk about his own hopes, dreams and challenges in the real estate business.

Jones Realty and Smith Realty have mutually agreed to enter into a discussion of future opportunities as related to the two companies. We mutually agree that the discussions and subsequent sharing of financial information is extremely personal and confidential. Bill Jones and Susan Smith will be the only individuals to access information deemed sensitive or confidential unless otherwise agreed to in writing. Such individuals will be required to sign a new confidentiality agreement.

We further agree not to discuss in any manner or use the information obtained for a period of 6 months from the date of this signed agreement. This agreement constitutes our desire to enter into freely, discussions regarding future opportunities for both parties.

_____   _____

Bill Jones   Date

_____   _____

Susan Johnson   Date

*Please seek legal counsel when drafting a specific agreement.

Sample Confidentiality Agreement   Fig. 4-B

EXPLORING THE FUTURE

This is precisely where you want to lead the conversation. Because this meeting is really A FACT-FINDING MISSION TO DETERMINE WHAT THIS PERSON WANTS TO DO WITH THE REST OF HIS/HER REAL ESTATE CAREER. You should not be talking price or terms at this point; it's too early. The key question that should be raised at the meeting is this: "John, Where do you see yourself in three years, or five years? If you didn't have this real estate company to run, what would you like to be doing?"

You may be surprised at the candid, straightforward answers you will get to that question. Often, people will come right out and tell you, "I'd like to be making more money," or, "I'd like to be spending less time running the office," or, "I'd like to be out of real estate." But you don't necessarily have to get an answer right away. Your objective in this meeting is threefold:

1) To get to know the person and the company a little better;

2) To get the candidate interested enough to agree to a second meeting (where there can be much deeper exploration, and at which point the candidate will probably be better prepared to answer some of your questions);

3) To end the meeting by asking this person to consider, over the next few days, the future and what they'd really like to do with their career.

THE SECOND MEETING

Having achieved all of that, set up that second meeting within the week — you don't want to lose the momentum you've already built. The second meeting is one of the most critical points in the entire acquisition process. Because this is the point at which the process really gets started. At the second meeting, you're going to move to the next stage by trying to get a true sense of what the candidate's wants and needs are — and what they plan to do with the rest of their career. And you are also going to begin to outline and explain how the acquisition process might work, if the two of you can come to an agreement.

As you begin to advance to this stage, and throughout all of your early discussions, it may be a good idea to be talking in terms of a PARTNERSHIP, not an acquisition. Even though some brokers may really want to get out of management or ownership, they don't want to feel that they're being taken over or that they're selling out. The talk should always center around "putting our two firms together." You want to show them the greater possibilities achievable of the two companies working together. And you want to make it clear that everyone can benefit from such a union — including the owners of both companies, and the agents and employees at both companies.

This particular style of business negotiation, in which the aim is to find the best solution for all parties involved, is also known as THE "WIN/WIN" APPROACH. I believe that it is a cornerstone to success in real estate negotiations — which is why you'll find many references to the "win/win" philosophy throughout this book. But it should be noted and understood that this is by no means the only way to approach negotiations with candidates. In fact, there are three basic types of negotiating approaches. (SEE FIG. 4-C; CHART ON THE 3 APPROACHES)

THE 3 APPROACHES

First, we have the "PASSIVE" approach, in which the buyer sim-

Fig. 4-C

ply puts out the word — through newspaper ads, direct mail, or word-of-mouth — that he's interested in acquisitions. The passive buyer would then wait for the candidate to come to him and initiate the negotiations. (If you have advanced to the stage of contacting individual candidates, then you've already moved beyond the passive approach.)

The second, and most common, approach is the "AGGRESSIVE" approach. An aggressive negotiator will contact each candidate and say something like this: "Would you like to sell your company? If you did sell, how much would you want for it?" Immediately thereafter, the haggling over price begins. The aggressive approach stresses winning (getting the lowest price) at all costs, and relies on manipulative negotiating techniques; for each point the seller raises, the buyer retaliates with a counterpoint.

But the problem with the aggressive approach is that it creates an adversarial relationship between buyer and seller right from the outset. That can ultimately damage your relationship with the company and its agents. And from my experience, it will almost always result in the buyer paying a higher price for a company. If you look at what happened in recent years to some of the larger financial companies that went on acquisition sprees in the real estate industry in the 1980s and early '90s, you find that they tended to approach acquisitions via aggressive, win-lose, purely financial negotiations; the results, in many cases, were that the acquisitions did not realize their true potential.

THE WIN/WIN PHILOSOPHY

The third approach — the one that I believe is most likely to result in successful acquisitions in the real estate business — lies somewhere in between passive and aggressive. It is the "win/win" approach. The win/win philosophy has become increasingly popular among the most cutting-edge thinkers in the business world today. The leading proponents of this philosophy include Dr. Stephen Covey, a top business consultant and the author of the best-selling book, "The 7 Habits of Highly Effective People," as well as Roger Fisher and William Ury, who teach negotiation at Harvard University.

According to Covey, "Most people tend to think in terms of dichotomies: strong or weak, hardball or softball, win or lose. But that kind of thinking is fundamentally flawed." As Covey notes, most business people are living in an "interdependent reality" — meaning that the people they deal with will continue to have some impact on them, even after a particular deal is finished. In a win/lose situation, Covey points out, the loser may not fulfill the contract; may carry grudges and battle scars into future dealings with you; and may spread that negative attitude to others. "In the long run, if it isn't a win for both of us," says Covey, "then we both lose."

Fisher and Ury, in their best-selling book "Getting To Yes," echo that philosophy. (Incidentally, I would strongly recommend that you read both "Getting to Yes" and Covey's "7 Habits." Though they're not about real estate, many of the principles in these books are applicable to our business). According to Fisher and Ury, "In most instances to ask a negotiator who's winning is as inappropriate as to ask who's winning a marriage." Instead, they advocate what is known as "principled negotiations" — in which negotiators focus on shared interests rather than opposing positions, and in which the two parties try to create options that will benefit everyone.

A good example of how this approach has been applied in a real estate acquisition involves the case of Ron Bell, a Florida broker who sold his company to Jim Porter, owner of ERA Old South Properties. When Porter first approached Bell, he didn't begin with standard negotiating offers — instead, he tried to find out what Bell's particular needs were. As it happened, Bell wanted to spend less time on business, and more time with his family. So Porter agreed that after the acquisition, Bell would serve as a vice president with the new company — but would only need to work part-time at the office. In this arrangement, says Bell, both parties got what they really wanted.

The win/win philosophy has caught on in a number of industries, including the car business; Detroit has recently undergone a dramatic shift toward responding to and solving customers problems, instead of just trying to force the latest car model down everyone's throats, i.e. we only make big cars so that's what you get. The auto company, the auto employee, and consumer are all more closely linked than ever in the research, design, and customization of individual cars. But I would contend that the win/win philosophy is perhaps ideally suited for the real estate business — where so much is dependent on human interaction and long-term relationships. As

Mark Masters says, "In the real estate business, win/win is really the only way an acquisition can be done successfully. You have to have goodwill on both sides after the deal — otherwise, you may end up losing key people and agents after the deal is completed."

CHANGING ATTITUDES

In some ways, it may be difficult for people engaging in real estate acquisitions to accept the win/win philosophy; after all, this is an extremely competitive ego-driven business, and many people tend to have a "beat-your-competitor-at-any-cost" syndrome. Oftentimes, you may find yourself in the position of acquiring a tough competitor that you've fought hard against for years; why should you want him to win? The answer is this: Once you begin the acquisition process, this person is no longer the enemy — now he/she is potentially your future partner.

The good news for real estate people is that in another sense, we're all used to practicing the win/win approach — with our customers. Whereas agents in years past tended to rely more on manipulative selling techniques, most of the better agents today have moved toward responding to needs and solving problems for the customers. And so, brokers who are embarking on an acquisition can borrow a lesson from what they've already learned in their dealings with customers — real success lies in building solid, long-term relationships.

But relationship-building is no easy matter; as we'll see in the next chapter, it takes time, effort, flexibility — and a willingness to look at everything from the other person's point of view.

CHAPTER FIVE

Relationship Building

The concept of relationship building is central to one's success in real estate acquisitions.

Your ability to develop a rapport with the seller based on mutual trust and respect is more than just a matter of goodwill; in the end, it can have a significant impact — either positive or negative — on the price that you pay for a company. Moreover, your success or failure in cultivating a relationship with the seller is likely to continue to have repercussions long after the acquisition is completed.

Why is this true? It relates directly to the particular nature of the real estate business. "When the owners of a real estate company sell, they aren't just selling a business — it may feel as if they're selling part of themselves," says Gloria Frazier of ERA American Realty. "For that reason, they want to sell to someone they're proud to be associated with — and someone they can trust." With rare exceptions, brokers truly care about the employees and agents that are part of their company; they also care about their reputation in the community. In most transactions that fail, the buyer has a customer mentality, similar to buying a car. The thought is that you are doing the salesman and dealer a favor by taking the car off their hands. Most successful transactions that involve the purchase of a business involve people that like each other. The parties have mutual respect and appreciation for the business aspects of the relationship, which is dramatically different than a customer approach.

TRUST EQUALS VALUE

And so, if a seller is convinced that you, the buyer, can be trusted to take care of his people, his good name and his lifetime investment — and that you might actually help the people and the operation to grow and prosper further — that translates to real value to the seller. And it can lower the price that the seller would be willing to accept.

The reverse is true, too. If a seller is selling to you reluctantly — perhaps because he/she doesn't have faith in the way you do business, or just doesn't like your style — that will put you in a weakened position as a buyer. You'll recall that we stressed earlier, in Chapter 1, that it's important to have your own house in order before you pursue acquisitions; brokers who don't treat their agents well, and don't service their customers well, are going to have a problem with acquisitions — because nobody wants to be acquired by this type of company.

If you are perceived by the seller in this negative way, that doesn't mean you can't acquire another company — but you will invariably have to pay more to acquire that company. And you'll probably have to pay more of that money upfront, too. Because no one will want to get involved in a deferred payment situation with you if they believe that there is potential that you might not be successful in retaining the agents after the acquisition.

Building a strong relationship with the seller has other ramifications beyond impacting on the price. It can influence the future success of the company after the acquisition, because it may determine whether the seller and other key players in that company work with you or against you once the transaction is completed.

EMPATHY IS THE KEY

How, exactly, do you build a strong relationship with a seller? It really begins with empathy — the ability to put yourself in someone else's shoes, and consider their needs. This is a somewhat radical concept in the world of negotiations, because so many people assume that negotiations are all about winning and looking out for number one. But the fact is, if you're going to be successful at relationship building, you will have to look at things from the seller's point of view.

And that's why relationship building often starts with finding out what the seller wants to do. There is a process that we will discuss, but it really can be defined as empathetic listening. Certainly you will need to tell the seller a lot about yourself, and your vision, and your goal for the company — how you plan to take it to the next level. But where you will really begin to build a relationship with that seller is when you ask that person the following questions: "Where would you like to be a year from now, or three years? What would you like to be doing? Do you want to stay in real estate? And if so, do you see yourself managing —- or would you rather go back to just selling?"

Determining the future of the seller may be fundamental to the sale. Typically, from the seller's perspective there are three steps to selling:

1) They must decide whether they want to sell;

2) They must decide what they want to do with their lives after selling;

3) They must decide whether they want to do all of this with you.

Questions one and two may be answered in reverse order, but in any case, the first two questions must be resolved before buyer and seller can agree on the third question.

EXPLORING THE FUTURE

Finding out what the seller wants to do after the sale may necessitate many conversations and some input and suggestions on your part. It won't necessarily come out the first time you meet, or even the second. There may be a need to build up trust before someone feels comfortable opening up to you, and sharing their dreams and hopes. You may have to help the process along, by probing this person's strengths and weaknesses, the things they like and don't like about the business. It may be as simple as asking, "What do you enjoy about running your office?"... and, "What drives you crazy about it?"

But it's also important to get the seller to think hypothetically; to move beyond the here-and-now and begin to consider the realm of possibilities. What if the seller wasn't bogged down by financial complications, or day-to-day administrative duties... what would this person be doing, if he/she were given freedom from existing restraints?

What you will find out, more often than not, is that the seller wants to get away from the day-to-day challenges that an owner/manager typically experiences in today's rough-and-tumble real estate market. In many cases, owners never really wanted to take on all these headaches in the first place. "Many of the most successful agents just naturally progress toward owning their own company," says Frazier. "It doesn't mean that they really wanted to do that, or that they're good at it. Often, they just seem to end up in that position."

But once they're owners, they may discover that they really don't like being responsible for everybody else's problems. And on top of that, they may actually be making less money than before: Many of these brokers were formerly top-producing agents whose personal revenues have declined since becoming an owner. Sound familiar to anyone?

At the same time, it often becomes clear to them where their real passions and strengths lie: They may realize that they really just love to sell. Or to train other agents. Or to work on marketing programs.

PLAY TO THEIR STRENGTHS

If you can identify where an owner's strengths and interests lie, you have a great opportunity to create a "second career" option for them within your company — and you'll probably strengthen your own operation in the process. Frazier has on two separate occasions acquired a company and kept the owner on as an agent. In both cases, those former owners have turned out to be top-selling agents; one of them just might be the strongest agent in Frazier's entire company right now, having closed 126 transactions last year.

Similarly, other buyers have filled various critical niches in their companies by bringing the seller on board after an acquisition (SEE CHECKLIST 5-A; ROLES SELLER MIGHT PLAY). Recently, Ken Ulsaker of ERA Five Star Properties in Burke, Va., acquired a company that specialized in commercial real estate; Ulsaker convinced the seller to stay on after the acquisition and help Five Star get its own commercial real estate division up and running. Meanwhile, Ron Bell, who — as mentioned in Chapter 4 — sold his successful company to ERA Old South Properties in

Pensacola, Fl., stayed on as a vice president and eventually was asked to take charge of all recruiting and sales management for the company.

Indeed, the seller may be the greatest single asset of the entire company that you are acquiring. Keep in mind that people who have run their own company are probably the best employees that you could hope for. They are generally more loyal — because while agents tend to suspect that owners are pocketing too much money and not doing enough work, a former owner understands how things really operate. They also appreciate the amount of effort and resources it takes to run a good company. Since they've been on both sides, as owner and employee, they can sometimes serve as a link to the rest of your staff. And they may be particularly important in maintaining stability among your new agents and employees after the sale. "It's very important to hang onto that key influencer in the company," says Mark Masters of ERA Prestige Homes. "If you lose that person, a lot of the agents may follow him out the door."

Roles Seller Might Play Within Your Company

1. Vice-President/ Sales Agent
2. Senior Sales Agent
3. Branch Manager
4. Assistant Manager
5. Recruiting Director
6. Property Manager/Commercial
7. Referral Director
8. New Homes Director
9. Training Director

Fig. 5-A

IMMEDIATE AND LONG-TERM NEEDS

While determining the future role of the seller in your company is one of the key aspects of building a relationship, there are other needs of the seller which should be addressed. In general, the seller's needs can be separated into two categories — LONG-TERM and IMMEDIATE. (SEE CHART, FIG. 5-B). The seller's "long-term needs" relate to career and future; these needs raise the question, "How am I going to get back into a productive lifestyle, pay for my child's college education, take that vacation, or maybe buy that boat that I've always wanted?" Satisfying long-term needs usually involves finding a way for the seller to make a living and enjoy the rest of his/her career.

But there are also "immediate needs," which tend to be more pressing in nature. Immediate needs usually involve some form of debt. There may be a phone bill or electric bill that must be paid, or they may have a credit line balloon in a month. And those debts may also be tied in with personal financial problems at home, as well as in the business. For the seller, these immediate needs raise the question, "How am I going to make it to next week?" (the heck with next year!)

With both immediate and long-term needs, if you can provide options and solutions, you can help the seller to be a more productive and profitable part of your company — and at the same time, you can lower the price that you will pay for a company. Oftentimes, buyers will say to a seller: "I'll give you $50,000 for your company but I don't want to mess with any of your problems. I don't want to deal with your copier, or your furniture, or your bills, or your lease." But that may be a big mistake on the part of the buyer.

> ### Difference Between Immediate and Long-term Needs
>
> *Immediate Needs:*
> Paying the rent
> Phone bill overdue
> Bank note coming due
>
> *Long-term Needs:*
> Figuring out what's next in his/her career
> How do I pay for my daughter's college
> I would like to spend more time with my family

Fig. 5-B

DEBTS ARE OPPORTUNITIES

On the contrary, debt relief may present a great opportunity for you to help the seller, move the deal forward — and save money in the process. Often, a seller will think, "I'd like to sell the company, but I can't because I owe too much," or "I'll never get back what I've put into it." But if you can come in and help solve that financial crunch — by say, helping to make a payment on a short-term note that is overdue — IT ALLOWS THE SELLER TO MOVE AHEAD WITH THE TRANSACTION AND WITH HIS/HER LIFE. And it gives you the opportunity to say: "Look, I'll take care of these problems; all you need to do is get back into real estate sales and tomorrow you can focus on being productive instead of worrying about bills. Let's get you back into the making money mentality." Naturally, the price you pay for a company would be lowered in relation to the amount of debt you assume — and often, you can actually come out far ahead. The fact is, the seller may be so anxious to walk away from these problems quickly that they may also be willing to walk away from thousands of dollars on the purchase price to relieve their current frustrations.

Keep in mind that as you are dealing with the seller's various needs, some may not be evident on the surface. We refer to these as the "UNDERLYING NEEDS" of the seller, and they may include everything from debts, to an impending divorce, to problems with the IRS, to agent defections. These are things that the seller won't necessarily talk about right away. Initially, they're apt to tell you they're tired of the business, or they're ready to retire, or they want to get back to sales. But keep in mind that perhaps the real reason for selling is that they're getting slapped with an IRS lien next week, or their agents have been walking out on them. As you cultivate a relationship with the seller and continue to probe, these issues will begin to surface. And when they do, you should once again view the problems as opportunities; it's a chance for you to help provide solutions.

CONSIDERATIONS TO NEVER FORGET

There are some other considerations, which I put under the heading of "Considerations to Never Forget." I must confess that over the years, I have at one time or another been burned on every one of these. (SEE CHECKLIST, FIG. 5-C).

SPOUSE. Topping the list is the seller's spouse. This person can turn out to be the wild card in your relationship with the seller. You may build a relationship with the seller, agree on a mutually beneficial future and decide that the company's worth $75,000 — and then the seller conveys this to the spouse, who becomes outraged. "What do you mean $75,000? We must have put $300,000 into this business? Who does this guy think he is?" At the root of the problem, often, is the spouse's misconceptions about the company. It's quite possible the seller hasn't told the spouse the whole truth about the condition of the business. The spouse may have an inkling that the money's been a little tight lately, but also has probably been

> **RELATIONSHIP BUILDING:
> CONSIDERATIONS TO NEVER FORGET**
>
> 1. Spouse- make sure he/she is aware of what's going on.
> 2. Find out if there is a partner or silent partner
> 3. Employees - remember, seller usually wants what's best for them.
> 4. Acknowledge the owner's hard work.
> 5. Help the seller save face.
> 6. Be humble about everything; don't boast.
> 7. Ask for advice.

Fig. 5-C

hearing over and over that, "The business is just about to turn the corner, everything's okay." Consequently, the spouse may think the business is stronger than it really is — and so a $75,000 offer can seem like an insult. And a hostile spouse can end up killing the transaction faster than you'd ever imagine. So you have to get the spouse involved as early as possible. From the outset, you should be asking the seller, "If we asked your spouse about this, what would they be likely to recommend to you? What does your family think about your real estate career? What future is in the best interests of you and your family?"

PARTNER OR SILENT PARTNER. You need to find out if the person you're dealing with is truly the decision-maker. I've been involved in talks with a seller only to find a silent partner come out of nowhere after the talks have begun; it may be an outside investor, or it may even be an agent at the seller's company. Whoever it is, that person must be fully involved in the process as quickly as possible — so there are no surprises later on.

EMPLOYEES. Similarly, the employees are a critical part of the mix. That's especially true of anyone who's been with the company for a number of years: the administrative person, the bookkeeper, or the receptionist. Sometimes they know more about running the office than the owner, and they're respected and trusted. So you must make sure that these people are foremost in your considerations, and that they're spoken of with respect. Many buyers going into an acquisition will say, "We're going to cut costs by getting rid of the receptionist." Well, maybe that receptionist has been there for 15 years and is loved by everyone at the company. Better to keep paying the receptionist and reduce the overall purchase price or expenses elsewhere. Generally speaking, brokers want what's best for their employees and agents; they want to be able to tell their people, "I've gotten the best opportunity for you guys, because now you'll have access to great training and resources." It's difficult for them to face loyal employees or agents they've recruited and say, "I'm sorry, but there's no room for you at the new company."

ACKNOWLEDGE THE OWNER'S HARD WORK. Almost all entrepreneurs feel that they've put their whole lives into the business, and it's usually true. They've given up weekends and vacations and they've missed their kids' ballgames, all so that they could be there for the business. Never underestimate the importance of this feeling of dedication and commitment in an owner. It's important to be empathetic and appreciative of all the work that has gone into the business. The owner's efforts over the years won't necessarily result in a higher selling price, but they should be acknowledged. You might say, "Look, no one could ever pay you back for the time and energy you've put in — but that has allowed you to get to this stage, and your payback is going to come over the next few years as you continue to be a major part of the new company's success. You created the foundation; now together we can take this company to another level."

Relationship Building

HELP THE SELLER SAVE FACE. It's so easy in an acquisition for the buyer to end up playing the role of the expert — the person who has all the answers, and who always knows best. You can find yourself saying things like, "If only you'd advertised more, or changed your commission schedule, or whatever, you'd have been more successful." Trust me, the seller does not want to hear this from you. There's no need to be critical or to second-guess — it's a surefire way to alienate people.

You don't know what the hot-buttons might be; I was once involved in an acquisition in a medium sized market in Florida, and we were very close to the closing date when my partner started talking to the seller about getting rid of the carpet, wallpaper and curtains, because the whole look of the office was just unacceptable. Well, it turned out the seller's wife had very recently redecorated. He didn't want to hear this criticism and practically threw us out of the office. You have no way of knowing how much effort and pride has gone into an operation, and what areas are sensitive, so you have to be very careful about criticizing anything. If you kick someone when they're down, you'll end up paying for it in some way.

ASK FOR ADVICE. Solicit the opinions and advice of the seller, to let them know you respect their expertise. Ask, "What would you suggest be done about the advertising, or the commission schedules? How would you handle the announcement? Maybe together we can figure out what's best for the new combined company." (By the way, these are great "concluding" questions as your talks with the seller wind down).

SELLING THE VISION

Though it's a good idea to ask for the seller's advice regarding future decisions and plans, you should also make it clear that you are coming into this acquisition with a current business strategy and the ability to execute it, as well as a clear vision for the company's future. You must convince the seller that if he/she becomes part of your growing organization, everyone will benefit; the new combined company will have greater market share, more listings, more visibility. There will be opportunities for the seller and his agents to make more money than ever before. And at the same time, the seller will have more freedom, and a chance to focus on doing what he/she enjoys. This is all part of what's known as "selling the vision" — and that's very important to entrepreneurs.

The major real estate franchise players that have grown rapidly in recent years have been extremely good at selling (and delivering on) the vision. Their approach to sellers has been: "We're going to create a nationwide real estate network, and have the best training available, and the best advertising, and the best overall support. And if you join this partnership, together we'd be able to do so much more than either of us would be able to do separately."

Finally, having discussed all the things you should say to a seller and all the questions you should ask, it's important to stress that you should not be doing any of this in a mechanical fashion. These are not merely techniques, designed to manipulate the seller and help you get what you want. Long-term relationships must be built on sincerity and trust. For instance, if you ask the seller's opinion just because that's something you're supposed to do, that kind of falseness will show through eventually. And when that happens and the seller realizes you've been manipulating him, that person will turn on you — and the partnership will fall apart. Manipulation and negotiating techniques may work in the short-run, but they won't fool people for very long.

A final thought to keep in mind as you are developing a rapport: BE PATIENT AND TRY TO KEEP AWAY FROM TALKING ABOUT NUMBERS. The seller is likely to push you for a dollar figure; the first thing they want to know in a conversation about acquisitions is, "How much are you going to pay me?" You should point out that it's premature to talk price or terms until you've established what your future relationship will be; once you both agree on future needs and goals, then together you can find a way to make the financial part work. But you should also assure them that when the time does come to establish a number, it will be fair to both sides and it will be arrived at together.

The fact is, before you can come up with the kind of figure that the seller is looking for, you're going to have to do some more homework. And that means you must proceed to the next stage — and our next chapter — which comes under the heading of "information gathering." But in the meantime, keep the conversation and the relationship moving forward. And remind the seller that as critical as the dollars are, it's equally important to agree on mutual goals, and visions of the future.

CHAPTER SIX

Information Gathering

People often ask, "How much information do you need before you're in a good position to buy a company?" The answer is: *As much as you can get your hands on.* In the information-gathering stage, you are trying to assemble as complete a picture as possible of the company that you are about to marry.

That means you should not approach this task in a one-dimensional manner — by focusing, for example, only on financial documents. Those documents will only tell part of the story. To really understand the culture and style of a company, you must look further, by gathering samples of the company's fact sheets, flyers, direct mail pieces, advertising, and even customer satisfaction surveys if possible.

This kind of "holistic" approach to information gathering is somewhat non-traditional; many acquisition people tend to concentrate only on financial information. Yes, the numbers are important, but first you need to learn as much as possible about the quality of the company's training programs and marketing capabilities and work ethic. This will begin to tell you if the company's culture and style of operation is compatible with yours. Eventually, the numbers will tell you what the company is actually worth. But if that compatibility isn't there to begin with — and if it seems unlikely that you can bring the company to your level — then there is really no point wading through all the financial data.

SEEKING COMPATIBILITY

Looking through the various company literature can tell you a lot about compatibility. If you see that a company is doing its fact sheets in a sloppy manner, that may not fit with the image you're trying to project. This doesn't mean you write the company off — because the solution may be simply a matter of providing the agents with better resources so that they can produce more professional letters and flyers. And in fact, the agents may jump at that opportunity: They may say, "Wow, now I'll have access to desktop publishing and a laser printer, which means I can really improve my own marketing efforts." So this could provide you an opportunity to get the new agents excited. Nevertheless, you should know upfront that you're going to have to make an investment in upgrading the quality and potential productivity of that office.

On the flip side, there's always the possibility that they're the ones who are producing embossed, slick, beautiful fact sheets — while yours are done in crayon. There are two ways of looking at this situation. Maybe you'll be able to learn from them and improve your own marketing. But if you're not prepared to come up to their marketing support level, that could lead to problems. Even if they've been getting a little too much marketing support, in terms of the broker spending money on fancy brochures that should have gone toward other areas, they have come to expect that support (even if the results don't justify the costs). If you come in and say that you're going to cut back on that, be prepared to deal with grumbling. It is a good idea to prepare a comparison of the products and services offered to each company's agents, and the correspond-

Sample Company Comparison

	Your Company	Candidate Company
1. Commission Schedules		
2. Administrative Support		
3. Opportunity Time System		
4. Long Distance Calls		
5. Voice Mail/ Messaging		
6. Direct Mail Support		
7. Postage		
8. Brochures/Supplies		
9. Signs		
10. Lock Boxes		
11. Computer System/Support		
12. Training		
13. Sales Meetings		
14. Caravans		
15. Dress Code		
16. Office Space-Agents		
17. Office Space-Conference Facilities		
18. Office Location		
19. Accounting/ Commissions paid		
20. After hours/weekend services		
21. Other		

Sample Company Comparison   Fig. 6-A

ing costs and compensation programs (SEE CHART, FIG. 6-A). In any case, you don't want to get blindsided by these kinds of operational differences; you should be aware of them going into the acquisition.

GATHERING DATA

As you begin to gather financial documents, you should have a checklist of all the information that you will need to collect You'll notice that this list includes a variety of information, including:

- Listing inventory by agent

- Start dates by agent

- Sales fall-out rates

- Managers' compensation

This information is fairly basic to any acquisition, though it should be noted that the amount of information you need will be determined, in part, by the size of the company you're acquiring. If it's a two-agent company with a very small number of listings, you can probably base your valuation formulas on the listing inventory, the pendings and the commission splits, without having to spend much time poring over income statements. But the larger the company, the greater the risk involved — and the more disclosure and research is required. It also should be noted that if you are doing a fold-in, there is less of a need for financial operating information — whereas if you're taking over existing operations, you will need to know what the monthly expenses currently are, and project what they're going to be. You need to get a sense of the cycles and trends, the peaks and valleys, of this particular business in recent times. At the end of this chapter there is a sample acquisition worksheet that will assist you in gathering basic information (SEE FIG. 6-E).

P&L STATEMENTS

Profit-and-Loss statements can help provide that picture. Annual P&L statements over the last three or four years will show you long-term trends. But it may be even more important to look at monthly statements, gathered over the past year or two; these will show you the more recent ups and downs — and just might tell you why the owner is interested in selling. Often a company may appear to the industry to be strong, but in reality the income's been going down in recent months — perhaps the top producers left four months ago and it's just starting to show up. The monthly reports can help you spot these trends; to clarify this, you can graph the revenue, expenses and net operating income on a monthly basis for the last two years. (SEE GRAPH, FIG. 6-B).

But keep in mind: You can't always tell how profitable a company is by the financial statements. Because much of what you see on a P&L statement may be the product of wishful thinking, clever accounting, or sometimes unintentional omissions on the part of the owner. Profit areas may be disguised as expenses, and expenses may be disguised as profit. For instance, let's say you come across two companies, and one is making $12,000 a year while the other is making $90,000 a year. Does that mean the $90,000 a year company is definitely worth more? Not necessarily; by the time you add back extraneous expenses that are actually profit, such as convention trips, the spouse's salary, the owner's car, and double market rent to the owner as landlord, it may turn out that the $12,000 company is actually more profitable.

Information Gathering

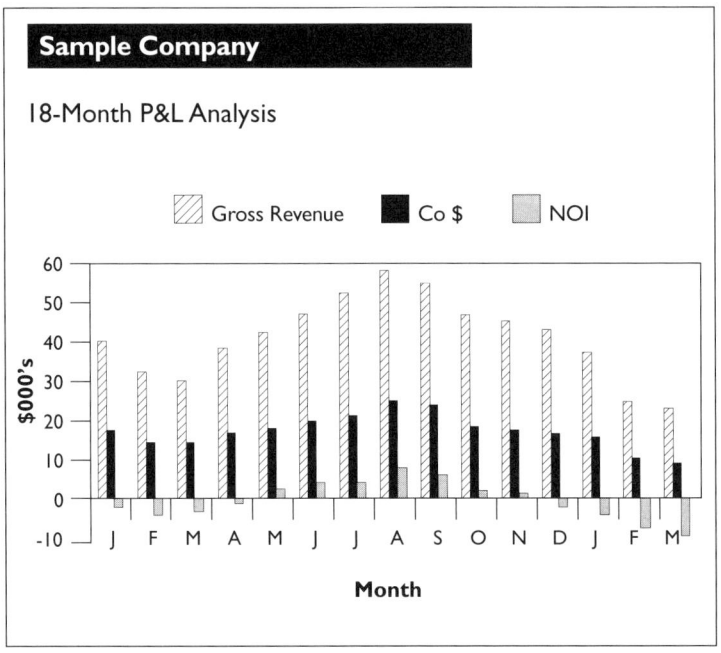

Fig. 6-B

MYSTERIES OF OWNER COMPENSATION/EXPENSE

The biggest variable in a P&L statement is probably owner compensation and expense. There is tremendous fluctuation from one company to the next; one owner may take 100 percent of their personal commissions out of the company, while another may leave 100 percent in the company to fund operations. Or they may take it out sporadically. Or they may take draws not related to management compensation or personal production. The owner may be compensated in a variety of ways, such as with cars or travel. This is all legal and legitimate and many people in real estate do it. But it's part of the reason why P&L statements in small companies are so varied that you can't completely trust them. There may also be a stack of payables in the drawer that are not reflected in the accountant's current compilation. Most statements are done on a cash rather than accrual basis, so if the owner hasn't paid $10,000 of current payables it would actually add $10,000 of profit to the current month.

You may need the help of an accountant to sort through the statements. But oftentimes, brokers can rely on their own experience to judge whether a particular expense seems appropriate. In any case, you may have to go through the statement line-by-line and ask the owner to explain items. And in particular, you must inquire about the owner's production, commissions and salary; when they make a sale, do they leave the income in to run the company? Who pays for the car, or the owner's travel? If the company owner also owns the building, is the company paying more or less than the market rate for rent? How are they compensated for management?

Ultimately, you should verify the financial statements by comparing them to the company's tax returns; you may find that the expenses and income they report to the IRS are dramatically different from the P&L statement. (You can save this verification for a later stage, perhaps when it's time to draw up a letter of intent; at the sensitive early stages, you don't want to seem as if you do not trust the seller.)

WHAT DOES THE OWNER OWN?

With regard to facilities, furniture and office equipment, it's critical that you find out exactly what the owner owns, and doesn't own. Tax return depreciation schedules are useful in telling you this, and they'll also tell you how old the furniture or equipment is (they typically tell you the date purchased for every asset and the purchase price). And you should ask to see all leases, obligations, and agreements. When it comes to phone systems, fax machines,

Information Gathering

copiers and the like, it's surprising how many owners just assume that the equipment belongs to them — when in reality, they're leasing all of it (it's not that the owner is lying; often a company administrator takes care of the leasing, so the owner isn't even aware of the difference between a lease or a lease with a purchase option, or a straight purchase on time.).

There are many horror stories about hidden leases. A few years back, a broker called me and told me about a company he'd acquired for $20,000 cash with everything included. The owner wanted to sell quickly, and be done with real estate; it looked like a great opportunity. And then about a month later, the bills started coming... all the furniture was leased, as were the copiers and fax machines. Because it was one of those rushed deals — "too good to pass up" — the buyer never really checked these things, he just took the seller's word that everything was owned and part of the deal. Look for other payables- homes magazine, newspapers, MLS dues, etc. The bottom line is, you have to find out about any leases, and actually get your hands on them and read them. In some agreements, there's a 10 or 20 percent fee to assign it or for someone else to use it, or the lease may have a mandatory purchase option, or stiff penalties for non-purchase. While you're looking for leases, also try to find out if any advertising contracts exist — with newspapers, radio, market magazines, etc. — and if so, what are their terms and conditions.

Also check on INDEPENDENT CONTRACTOR AGREEMENTS the seller may have signed with his/her agents: Are they legal, and are there any obligations you should know about? You'll probably want to have all the agents sign your own independent contractor agreement. Finally, check for membership or association contracts: Look at their board memberships, whether they're in franchises or referral networks, and even trade associations. For the most part, these won't be a problem, but sometimes membership contracts will require that an ongoing fee be paid or there is a financial penalty for early termination.

AGENT PRODUCTION

Agent production is an area that requires close scrutiny. If you look at the company's tax schedules, you can see income broken down on an agent-by-agent basis. "You want to see if production is evenly distributed — or whether you have a couple of people who are carrying the company," says Gloria Frazier. If the latter is true, then you're in a higher-risk situation, because you are dependent on hanging on to those key people. If possible, you should be looking at agent production over the last two or three years — so that you can see who's gaining and losing momentum. And find out the start dates of agents so you can distinguish between the production of veterans and newcomers, and so you can get a sense of agent retention and the turnover rate.

LISTING INVENTORY

If you ask a broker how many listings they have, they may say 75 — but in actuality they may have 100, or they may have 50. Again, it's not that they're misleading you; they might not know exactly what their current listing count and their inventory is. And that's very important, whether you're buying a fold-in or an existing operation. You'd want to see the listing inventory over the last 2 years, and also on an agent by agent basis. "You're looking for a good mix of saleable property in the inventory, as opposed to just a lot of numbers that have not translated to sales. And you want to see if the list prices are lower or higher than the average for that area," Frazier says. "You have to consider not just the number of listings but the salability of each of those listings."

And pay close attention to the expiration dates, which can tip you off to agent problems: You probably are already familiar with the pattern, but when agents are planning to leave, they often have all their listings expire at about the same time. In terms of pending sales, you need exact dates, times, when they're going to close, and how much they're closing for — because you are going to base part of the valuation formula on that.

GOING BY THE BOOK

Policy manuals will tell you a number of important things about the company, such as:

- Commission splits

- Opportunity time

- Referral policy

- Advertising policy

- Expense contributions

(SEE CHART ON POLICY MANUALS, FIG. 6-C).

But beware: The policy manual may not be totally in line with reality at that company. For example, the splits may be arranged on a sliding scale through the year — so that if you're buying in mid-year, you're going to have to bear the brunt of it in November and December. And the major problem with policy manuals is that companies may not always follow their own manuals closely — and sometimes don't follow them at all. So it's important to find out what the individual commission splits and overall compensation agreements are, particularly where the top producing agents are concerned.

> ### POLICY MANUALS
>
> | *What the policy manual tells you* | *... and doesn't tell you* |
> |---|---|
> | Standard commission splits | Special arrangements made with individuals regarding splits, reimbursements, etc. |
> | Opportunity time | |
> | Advertising policy | How often the policy manual is followed |
> | Expense policy | |

Fig. 6-C

You may have to go down the list and ask about each individual agent. Find out not only about the split, but whether there are other perks offered to the agent in lieu of a higher split. For instance, a particular agent might be on a 50/50 split, but may also receive additional advertising and perhaps a part-time assistant secretary, paid for by the broker. You have to uncover what all of these special arrangements are, because the broker won't necessarily tell you outright.

WHO DOES WHAT?

Job titles don't necessarily tell you what people really do at the company. Oftentimes, a person's responsibilities at a company go well beyond their title. Is the administrative person actually running the office? Is the spouse doing the bookkeeping? And how about the broker's duties — do they encompass everything from typing memos to going to open houses? If the broker was performing additional duties and not taking a salary for it, that means after the acquisition you may have to add a manager that in your market you're going to have to pay $40,000 for — which comes straight out of the profits. It's important to know these things because it will tell you about your own staffing needs after the acquisition. It is important to identify how all the current functions will be performed in the new company, who will do them, and how much they will cost.

"NEVER FORGET" LIST

Finally, we come to another checklist, which I call "Considerations to Never Forget." This should be referred to as you're gathering information, because it's so easy to overlook these:

1) *POLICY MANUAL VS. REALITY:* As mentioned earlier, the two can be worlds apart. So it's important to look at the manual, but don't take it as gospel.

2) *LEASED EQUIPMENT VS. PURCHASED:* Don't assume that everything is owned, particularly furniture, phone systems, and office equipment.

3) *ASSIGNMENT CLAUSES:* If equipment or property is leased, and if they assign it, there may be a large assignment or a "re-upping" — you may be required to take another three

or four year contract, so be on the lookout for that. With regard to occupancy leases, keep in mind that some don't allow sub-letting; or may charge for assignment of the lease; or may have an out clause for the landlord with the change of ownership.

4) *RE-ALLOCATE STRANGE EXPENSES:* These may include going to numerous trade conferences (vacations) and writing it off, or season tickets to ball games that are used for "marketing purposes" and written off. If you're going to continue to do that, fine — but if not, add it to potential profit.

5) *NEW EXPENSE:* Determine what level of current, additional, or re-allocated expenses will be needed to achieve your desired growth and return, including when you will need the expense and where it will go.

6) *BE CAREFUL OF OWNER'S PRODUCTION, COMMISSIONS, SALARY, COMPENSATION:* As discussed earlier, this is an area of great concern, particularly with smaller companies. You must ask specific questions of the owner, i.e., "Of your income last year, how much was from personal production?" "How did you receive your compensation from the company (draw, bonus, weekly)?" "What portion was for personal production, management compensation, and profit?" These questions are important, because in the event that broker leaves, you must know how much of the company's revenue was directly attributable to his or his spouse's commissions.

7) *ANALYZE LISTING INVENTORY:* You should look closely at expiration dates, inventory mix, and salability. You have to look at expirations on an agent by agent basis and the company by historical information and your market knowledge.

Information Gathering   85

8) *FINALLY, PREPARE A "NEW COMPANY" PRO FORMA:* By the pro forma we're simply talking about an educated guess (projection) of what you think is going to happen with revenues and expenses over the next year. (SEE SAMPLE PRO FORMA, FIG. 6-D). Working from the P&L statements, your knowledge of the individual agents, and your sense of the combined synergy between the two companies, come up with your best estimate of what the expenses will be over the next year, along with your best estimate of the income. If you find, for example, that your expenses are going to be $50,000 and your income $60,000, you're left with $10,000 profit. Now the question you must ask yourself is, HOW MUCH AM I WILLING TO PAY RIGHT NOW FOR THAT $10,000 OF NET NEXT YEAR AND THE SUBSEQUENT PROJECTED PROFIT FOR THE YEARS AHEAD? The answer to that question, along with the valuation formulas that we will examine in the next chapter, will help determine the price that you ultimately will pay. The pro forma can also be used as a cash flow management tool to determine the amount and timing of capital requirements.

A final thought: At this stage, you should take your time and make sure that you gather all the information you need. When you're in the acquisition mode, there's a temptation to want to push ahead quickly. And sometimes you'll come across a deal that appears too good to be true; the seller will tell you, "I need to close by next week and you'll get a deal of a lifetime." But nine times out of ten, such deals are too good to be true, and something's wrong. We've had a broker who bought a company on a Friday, only to find on Monday that the IRS had come in and put a lien on everything. So don't get rushed at this stage; you have to do your research thoroughly before you will be ready to proceed to the next critical stage — determining what the company is really worth.

New Company Pro Forma (000'S)

Month	1*	2*	3*	4	5	6	7	8	9	10	11	12	Annual
GROSS REVENUE	$28	26	28	32	40	44	55	70	65	48	40	39	$515
DIRECT COST	$17	16	17	19	24	26	33	42	39	28	24	23	308
CO $	$11	10	11	13	16	18	22	28	26	20	16	16	$207
EXP	$18	18	14	14	15	15	16	17	16	15	15	15	$188
NOI	<$7>	<8>	<3>	<1>	1	3	6	11	10	5	1	1	$19

* Example includes 1/3 of pending sale company dollar income of seller going to seller

Fig. 6-D

Sample Acquisition Worksheet
Company Profile

Name: _____
Address: _____
Phone: _____
Ownership: _____ % Owned: _____
                       _____ % Owned: _____
                       _____ % Owned: _____
                                    Sole Proprietor _____
                                    Corporation   _____
                                    Partnership   _____
Managing Broker: _____

<u>Primary Business:</u>
New   _____ %
Resale   _____ %
Condos   _____ %
Commercial Property   _____ %
Management   _____ %
Retail   _____ %

<u>Branch Locations:</u>
List by Address/Approximate Sq. Ft./Lease or Own/Monthly Rent/Time Remaining
_____
_____
_____
_____
_____

Fig. 6-E

Operational Summary

Year	# Agents	# Listings	# Sides Closed	Company Dollar
YTD thru ___	_____	_____	_____	_____
1995	_____	_____	_____	_____
1994	_____	_____	_____	_____
1993	_____	_____	_____	_____

Financial Summary

	YTD thru ___	*1995*	*1994*	*1993*
Gross Commissions	_____	_____	_____	_____
Commissions Paid Agents	_____	_____	_____	_____
Company Dollar	_____	_____	_____	_____
Operating Expenses	_____	_____	_____	_____
Net Profit (Loss)	_____	_____	_____	_____

Personal Compensation

% of Time		*1995*	*1994*	*1993*
_____	Commission Income	_____	_____	_____
_____	Management Compensation	_____	_____	_____
	Profit Distributions	_____	_____	_____
	*Perks & Benefits	_____	_____	_____

*Please explain: _____
_____
_____
_____

Fig. 6-E

Agent Productivity

List Top 10 Agents, Prior Year Activity (No Agent Names Requested, Include Yourself if Applicable).

Date started in the business/with company	# of Listings Taken	# of Sides Closed	1099 Earnings
#1			
#2			
#3			
#4			
#5			
#6			
#7			
#8			
#9			
#10			

Major Lease/Company Loans:
(purpose, remaining term, monthly payment)
1) _____
2) _____
3) _____

Litigation Pending (if any):
_____
_____

Fig. 6-E

Agent Support

1) A. Attach copy of your commission schedule:
   B. Attach copy of your policy manual

2) Briefly explain company policies on expenses:
   - Phone/long distance   _____
   - Postage   _____
   - Advertising   _____
   - Direct Mail   _____
   - Other marketing materials _____
   - E&O   _____

3) Your referral system

4) Availability and cost (to agents) of new and experienced agent training

5) Manager owner competition with agents

6) Sales Meeting Frequency and Content

7) Type of Automated Support Supplied

8) Other General Information
   1) Staff Support/List Number of Individuals (indicate branch if appropriate), Length of Employment & Annual Compensation
      - Owner   _____
      - Manager (s) _____
      - Secretary   _____
      - Relo   _____
      - Reception   _____
      - Bookkeeping _____

Fig. 6-E

2) Information Systems/Indicate if available and if manual or computer
    Operating Reports   _____
    Listings Management   _____
    Financial Reports   _____
3) Do you Currently Offer
    Home Warranty   _____
    Home Purchase   _____
    Trade-In   _____

_____   _____

Pending Business (as of ___/___/___)

Listings (Attach current listing inventory)
Number in Inventory   # _____
Total $ in Value $ _____
Net Office Commission Rate   _____%
Commissions to Company After Agents are Paid $ _____
Days on Market   _____
Average % Sold   _____%

Contracts Pending
(Attach Pending Summary by date)

Total Contracts Escrowed   # _____
Commissions Due Company After Agents are Paid $ _____

Capital Assets
Indicate either book value or estimated current market value (circle one).
Furniture & Fixtures $ _____
Telephone Systems $ _____
Computer (s) $ _____
Land & Buildings $ _____
Other _____
                                    Total $ _____

Fig. 6-E

CHAPTER SEVEN

Potential Fit and Company Valuation

If acquiring a real estate company happened to be a science and nothing more, then this would be the stage at which you would be presented with a foolproof formula for determining the value of the seller's company. You would then apply that same equation to each and every acquisition in the future. It would all be so simple.

But the acquisition process in real estate isn't nearly as formulaic as that. Certainly, science and formulas are a part of it — and in this chapter you will be introduced to several formulas that are designed to help you sort through the uncertainties of company valuation. But those formulas, in and of themselves, will not provide the key to a successful acquisition — because while they may help you to place a theoretical dollar value on a company, it's important to remember that valuation formulas are generic. Although they can be invaluable in helping you assess your opportunity, they apply the same equations to every situation — when in fact every company and each acquisition is unique.

Formulas don't address the specific needs of a particular buyer and a particular seller. They overlook the "HIDDEN VARIABLES" — which we'll discuss shortly — that can influence any deal. They often don't address the very real possibility of a "culture clash" after the sale — which can render all of your formula-based projections completely moot. And they usually don't deal with the critical issue of risk — something that is inherent in any acquisition but which can, and should, be managed and shared effectively to avoid disasters. So, in this chapter, while presenting a variety of formulas to assist you in the process, we will also deal with these other issues that are central to determining how much you pay and how you pay it.

NO "RIGHT" PRICE

If there's one key point that should be stressed at the outset of any discussion about value, it is this: There is no "exact price" for any given company. If someone tells you your company is worth $108,542 there is a good chance they are guessing. The reason there can be no true consensus of what any company is worth has to do with the nature of the real estate business, which is localized, specialized, and dependent on all sorts of intangibles. Hence, the same company can be worth $100,000 to one buyer and $200,000 to another. Similarly, I've seen buyers pay as much as 10 or 12 times a company's pretax earnings and end up with a successful acquisition — while another buyer pays 3 times pretax, but ends up with an unsuccessful acquisition.

So it's important to view the formulas that will be presented in this chapter as guidelines; they can help you set the parameters of value, at which point the subtle and flexible art of negotiation gets started.

BEGIN WITH THE FIT

As we've discussed earlier, the success of an acquisition depends greatly on what happens after you purchase the company. For the implementation stage to go smoothly, you must ensure that the company you're acquiring is "a good fit" with your own. In the previous chapter, we noted that company flyers, advertising and literature can provide early clues as to whether a company's culture is compatible with yours. But as you reach the stage of actually valuating a company, it's critical that you determine just how well that particular company is going to fit with yours. All the valuation formulas in the world won't help you if you eventually find yourself in the midst of a culture clash between two organizations that were never meant to be married.

Just ask Len Davis (whose name has been changed here), a California-based broker who saw one of his acquisitions turn into a small-scale "civil war" right inside his own office. "We acquired a company that had a much looser management style than ours," says Davis. "Everyone at that company did their own thing, skipped meetings and dressed the way they wanted. Meanwhile, we were trying to create a more upscale image with our company." The result was resentment between agents on the two sides, leading to eventual defections of both old and new agents. Says Davis: "If I go looking for another company in the future, I'm going to look much more closely at the culture of that company to make sure they're compatible."

MISMATCHED PERSONALITIES

What causes cultures to be mismatched? As we all know, every real estate operation has a distinct personality — often a reflection of the broker. You can tell a lot about culture from the broker and the way he operates. Sometimes, for example, you'll find that company A is built around team players and a supportive, open environment, while company B is filled with agents who are looking out for themselves. (SEE CHART ON CULTURES, FIG. 7-A).

Potential Fit and Company Valuation 95

While each approach may be successful on its own, if you put these two companies together, the results can be destructive; it's not surprising to see the non-team players drive out some of the better team players. If the acquired agents don't show up for sales meetings, don't cover for each other when they're out of town, and don't observe rules of good conduct when it comes to going after walk-in customers, they can begin to poison your culture — and once your own team players see that kind of atmosphere developing, they head for the hills.

So it's important to ask the seller specific questions relating to culture, i.e., how are your people at attending sales meetings? Do they support you when you have problems as a group? And do they work well and support each other? Is customer satisfaction a priority? Your own associates may be a good source of information; their paths have probably crossed those of the seller's agents. And often, the level of professionalism shown by agents when dealing representatives of a competing company is a good indication of how they work with fellow agents within their own company.

Cultures

Team A

Willing to attend meetings, rallies, etc...
Wears a jacket to work
Aggressive about getting business
Likes high-tech equipment

Team B

Likes to be left alone
Wears jeans
Waits for phone to ring
Likes the old typewriter

Fig. 7-A

IS IT WORTH IT?

At some point, after you've gotten a feel for the culture, you must ask yourself the following: "Can I make this integration successful? And what effect will it have on my agents, my staff — and on me?" This should be considered from both an operational and financial standpoint: Can the receptionist and other support services handle the additional people (will you need new phone lines, another copier or MLS terminal)? How much money and time is it worth to you to bring both sides together and keep everyone happy? Even if the cultures fit well together, it's a lot of work bringing them together. But keep this in mind, too: If you weren't doing the acquisition, your only means of achieving comparable growth would be to do a mass recruiting of agents — which also requires a great deal of time, diligence, and effort. In comparison, an acquisition — even with all the headaches of marrying cultures — can seem like a jump-start compared to recruiting one agent at a time.

Is incompatibility a deal-breaker? Not necessarily. Because you can change someone who has not had the proper support and services. And it may be that only a few of the agents are problematic, and the rest are fine. But if the incompatibility problems involve the lead agents, who are the most visible and vocal of the group, you have to factor that into your evaluation. That is almost certainly going to make your transition more complicated and difficult. And the more difficult you expect the transition to be, the higher your risk is, and the lower your purchase price should be.

THE FORMULAS

Having determined that a company is a good fit, it's time to begin evaluating companies based on the numerical information you have gathered; at this point, you may begin to apply one or more of the Basic Valuation Formulas. There are several formulas that are widely used today, and they have different advantages and disadvantages.

The following are some of the most widely-used formulas:

1) Book Value Approach

2) Per-Agent

3) Per-Listing

4) Replacement Valuation

5) Income Approach (which can be broken down into several different formulas).

THE BOOK VALUE APPROACH is perhaps the most conventional way to place value on a company, though it may be more appropriate in industries other than real estate. With this method, the buyer tallies up all of the seller's various company assets, and places a dollar value on the worth of these assets. If you were to look at prices paid for real estate companies, you'd tend to find that buyers are generally paying about 2 to 2.5 times the book value of the assets (equipment, listing inventory, pendings). The building value, if appropriate, is more easily valued separately.

The problem with basing valuation on assets is that you're not factoring in the most important elements in the purchase — the quality of the agents, the goodwill of the company, its potential to turn a profit, and so on. One company may just have had more money to start with and paid cash for their equipment versus another that leased. This formula would favor the first. One variation is to use what is referred to as an "ASSET SUMMATION

APPROACH," which not only tallies tangible assets, but also attempts to estimate the value of intangibles, such as goodwill, performance of agents and even external market factors, such as development trends in the community. In this model, the total value of the company would be the sum of net tangible assets, current listings and pendings and the goodwill from future net productivity of the sales staff. But this approach necessitates that you rely heavily on rough estimates for the intangibles, and still places too much emphasis on the tangible assets. In reality, hard assets are less important than ever in today's real estate acquisitions — because many companies don't even own the buildings in which they operate, or the equipment they use.

PER-AGENT VALUATION of a company determines value strictly on the basis of the single most important of assets — the agents. Some buyers pay a flat price per agent when acquiring a company; for example, they might pay $1,000 per agent, with $2,000 paid for the higher producers. But how do you arrive at such a figure? It's usually based on other comparable acquisitions in the same market. If you found that ABC Realty conducted four acquisitions in your market, you could add up all the numbers and come up with an average number that they paid per agent. Such analysis tends to be more reliable when you're dealing with your own numbers, working from prior acquisitions. (Note: When analyzing prices paid per agent, make sure you're looking at "full time equivalent" agents, as opposed to part-timers).

PER-LISTING VALUATION. The same approach that is used in analyzing per-agent costs can also be applied to listings: Based on other comparable acquisitions in the market, you can determine how much is being paid per listing, and that can serve as a guideline. Many companies will pay anywhere from a low of a 20 percent referral fee for listings as they close, to a high of 100 to 150 percent of company dollar for listings as they close. This approach is particularly common with smaller acquisitions. For an example on calculating the value of the listing inventory, see accompanying form (FIG. 7-B)

CURRENT LISTING INVENTORY VALUATION

Current Listing Inventory Dollar Volume		$ 9,100,000
Sales Rate		X .80 (D)
	=	$ 7,280,000
Times % of Asking Price		X .93 (E)
	=	$ 6,770,400
Times Net Office Commission %		X .013 (C)
	=	$ 88,015.20
Times Turnover Rate		X 3 (A)
Divide by 12 Months		/ 12
Projected Monthly Income from Listings	=	$ 22,003.80
Divide by % of Income for Listings		/ .66 (B)
Projected Total Monthly Income	=	$ 33,339.09
Less Monthly Expense		-$24,400
Monthly Profit (Loss)	=	$ 8,939.09

Time in Months Before Income is Received:
$$\frac{(90) \text{ Days on Market} + (30) \text{ Processing Time}}{30} = 4 \text{ months}$$

Fig. 7-B

100   ACQUIRING PROFIT

A: Turnover Rate

The Turnover Rate forecasts the number of times in one year you should receive the projected value of your inventory. It is calculated by dividing 365 (the days in a year) by the Average Days your inventory is on the Market before it is placed under contract. This measurement reflects the quality of the inventory relative to the competitor's properties that are attempting to be marketed and the speed with which action is taken to make competitive adjustments.

B: Percent of Income from Listings

This performance indicator shows how adequately your inventory meets your buying customer's needs and how willingly your Agents seek cooperation when they do not have what the customer wants. It is calculated by dividing your Company Dollar earned on the sale of your listings by your Total Company Dollar. This measurement is also used to project your Total Commissions.

C: Net Office Commission

This performance indicator expresses the Company Dollar as a percentage of the Sales Price. It is calculated by dividing the Company Dollar (i.e. Gross Commissions less the amounts paid to Agents and other Brokers) by the Sales Volume. It reflects the relationship between Gross Commission, Agent splits and the amount of transactions where the Listing and Selling Agents are both in one company.

D: Sales Rate

This performance indicator may be calculated using listing units or their dollar volume. Sales Rate is determined by dividing the listings sold (closed) by the total listing removed from inventory (i.e. closed, expired, canceled, or withdrawn by the owner) during a given period. It reflects the quality of the inventory relative to the competitor's properties that are attempting to be marketed.

E: Percent of Asking Price Received
This performance indicator may be calculated by dividing the sale price of a listing by its most recent asking price prior to the acceptance of an offer by the seller. It reflects the quality and frequency of competitive adjustments made after the listing was taken.

THE REPLACEMENT VALUATION APPROACH takes a whole different approach from asset measurement. Here, the buyer attempts to calculate how much it would cost to duplicate or recreate the seller's company if the buyer were starting from scratch — building a new facility, recruiting and hiring new agents, and so forth. Most professional appraisers in other industries use this approach (i.e., residential appraisers).

But this approach can be subjective and imprecise. For example, there may be elements of a company that would be difficult or impossible to recreate — such as its reputation in the community, its precise office location, or its key managers. In reality, you cannot duplicate another company.

Still, the replacement valuation model is useful in showing you the alternative to pursuing that acquisition. Once you calculate the numbers, it will probably make you want to pursue the acquisition more than ever. Because you find that start-up costs — including everything from construction of facilities and purchasing of furniture and office equipment to heavy recruitment and training costs, various license and membership fees, and heavy initial advertising costs — are significant. And that doesn't even begin to factor in the time and effort required in a start-up. In a typical market, it might take a $70,000 cash investment plus a lot of hard work to replace a company generating $100,000 in company dollar. Meanwhile, if you were to acquire that same company, you'd probably pay far less. So it's fair to say that the replacement formula provides you with a number that represents the upper limit on the value of a firm. It's what many appraisers use as a worst-case scenario: Usually, an acquisition is going to be far more cost-efficient than a start-up.

THE INCOME APPROACH is, I believe, the best way to evaluate a company. These formulas provide a sense of what a company is worth, based on income; they consider assets of that company only to the extent that those assets impact on income. You might say that this approach cuts to the chase — because ultimately, what you are going after is the future income and profitability of the company that you're acquiring. The income formulas can best help you to answer the question that is central to the acquisition process: If I pay x amount for this company, how much will I get back and when? The following are probably the three most widely used income formulas.

> *1) MULTIPLY THE NET PRE-TAX EARNINGS BY FOUR TO SIX TIMES.* Using this formula, if you have a company with $50,000 of net operating income, the range of your total purchase price would be between $200,000 and $300,000. It seems simple enough, but there is one caveat: It seems that everyone has a different definition of what constitutes pre-tax earnings, depending on how they allocate the various "strange expenses." For the same company, pre-tax earnings could be $10,000 or $50,000 or $75,000, depending on how they do the books. For this formula to work you must re-allocate the income and expense statement to fairly reflect the profit.
>
> *2) MULTIPLY THE EARNINGS BEFORE INTEREST AND TAXES (EBIT) BY AN ANNUAL NET MULTIPLIER OF THREE TO FOUR.* For those not familiar with the term, the annual net multiplier is simply the inverse of the capitalization rate; when you do the pro forma, if the capitalization rate you are seeking is 25 percent, you're dealing with a multiplier of four (which means that you believe the net operating

income will give you your investment back in four years). If a company's EBIT is $10,000 and the capitalization rate is 25 percent, then the multiplier is four — and so the value would be $40,000. Most of the major players are now working with a multiplier of 3 to 4; any investment that takes 5 years or more to recoup is considered very risky. This formula changes based on your desired return and risk acceptance level.

3) PAY 25 TO 50 PERCENT OF ANNUAL COMPANY DOLLAR. This is the formula I tend to use most; IT IS THE MOST ACCURATE SIMPLY BECAUSE IT IS BASED ON A SOLID AND VERIFIABLE NUMBER (as mentioned earlier, with net figures you're on shakier ground because the seller can hide expenses). Annual company dollar, by the way, is the revenue of a company after agents commissions have been paid.

If the seller's annual company dollar figure is $100,000, you should be paying $25,000 to $50,000 as a total purchase price — meaning that it includes all basic furniture and equipment needed to conduct business.

That percentage may seem low to the seller, based on all the time and money that the seller may have put into the company over the years. In building that $100,000 company, the seller may have invested $200,000 over the years. But what matters to you, the buyer, is what will come out of the company in the immediate future, in terms of earnings. To put it in proper perspective, you're paying for an opportunity to earn perhaps $10,000 in net operating income next year.

It's no different from other industries, in which the share price is directly related to net earnings; McDonald's may have earned billions and billions over the years, but if they're not profitable right now, or investors feel they won't be in the near future, the share price and net worth is going to decline. So the concept you must get across to the seller is that you're empathetic and appreciative of all they've put into the company, but nevertheless, the company's value can be based only on present and future earning potential. You might pose the following question to sellers who overvalue their own companies: "If you were me, how much would you pay for the opportunity to earn X amount in net operating income next year?" Generally speaking, as you go along, you will find that you must very gently educate the seller on value and on the legitimacy of the formulas you are using.

To see how these different formulas compare when using the same set of figures, see the accompanying comparison chart (FIG. 7-C).

EXAMPLE:

Annual company dollar: $100,000 *Pretax earnings: $10,000*

A. 4 to 6 times pretax earnings	$40,000 to $60,000
B. Annual net multiplier of 3 to 4	$30,000 to $40,000
C. 25-50 percent annual co. dollar	$25,000 to $50,000
ESTIMATED VALUE	$35,000 TO $50,000

Fig. 7-C

COMING TO TERMS

While the valuation formula can provide a target value range to work with, perhaps the most critical aspect of the transaction is the terms that you agree upon with the seller, which will dictate how and when the price is paid. If, for example, you determine that our example company is worth $50,000, you might pay $10,000 at closing, and another 20 percent in 30 to 60 days as the pendings close, and another 20 percent at end of year one, and the balance over the next two years.

The terms and price are interrelated; to get the better of one, you must give up some of the other. Whether you pay a premium price or a minimum price for a company will often depend upon the terms of the deal.

While there's a natural tendency to want to pay the lowest price, in real estate acquisitions getting the right terms may actually be more important than getting the lowest price. Conceivably, a buyer could acquire a company at a "bargain" price by agreeing to pay all the money upfront, with no terms. But with a real estate company, that is extremely risky — because the seller's agents may defect shortly after the sale, and the buyer will have paid for a company that is almost worthless.

RISK-SHIFTING

Because such risks are inherent to real estate acquisitions, it's important for buyers to protect themselves via the process of "risk-shifting", wherein the buyer structures the terms of the transaction so that risk is shared by buyer and seller. To shift risk to the seller, payment to the seller is disbursed over time, and may also be tied to the performance of the seller's agents; a minimal amount of cash is paid upfront. While risk-shifting may raise the overall price that you pay, it's the preferable way to buy a company. If the agents do the performance you're hoping for, then you're willing to pay a premium price   and if they don't, you're protected or at least your monetary risk is reduced (SEE RISK-SHIFTING GRAPH, FIG. 7-D).

Even though the price may rise as you shift risk to the seller, that doesn't necessarily mean you'll pay more in the end. Since the payout is guaranteed only on production, and is based on the earnings of acquired agents, there is a good chance that you will not end up paying out the full amount — because some of those agents are bound to leave, due to ordinary turnover.

Fig. 7-D

LESS UPFRONT

In shifting risk to the seller, you would keep the upfront payment to a minimum (10 to 20 percent). Some buyers don't want to pay any money upfront, but you must keep in mind that the seller may have short-term financial needs that must be addressed — such as debts or unpaid bills. If you can come up with enough cash to solve those problems, you may be able to help the seller get out of a financial bind and become a productive part of your team. That is money well-spent. But keep this general rule in mind: The more you're paying upfront, the greater your risk — so you have to be more confident in your analysis of the company and more certain of your ability to run that company. And also remember that the more you pay upfront, the less assured interest the seller has in the success of the company after the deal; if they get most of their money early, they may be less likely to help you in year two or three.

Though sellers may be resistant to long-term payouts, there are advantages for everyone in deferred payment. To the seller, in most cases it can result in tax savings (if the seller gets all the money from the sale at once, he/she will pay more taxes than if it's spread over three years), as well as providing continuity of income over a two or three year period. And of course, the seller has a chance to make more money on the sale in the long run, particularly if the agents stick around and produce. The benefits of deferred payment to the buyer are obvious: Less risk, less cash tied up, and more support and loyalty from the seller.

NEGOTIATING VARIABLES

As you work out the final price and terms of the transaction, there are a number of basic negotiating variables at your disposal; these can be used to raise or lower price accordingly. (SEE VARIABLES CHART, FIG. 7-E). Buyers can use any one of these exclusively, or more typically may use several variables in some combination. The basic tools include:

• *CASH UPFRONT:* No more than 20 percent, which is high;

the average is more in the range of 0 to 10 percent.

- *PENDINGS* (0 to 100 percent of company listing): Sellers often want to retain their income from the pendings inventory; the buyer, meanwhile, wants to make it a part of the purchase and pay it out as they close. Some buyers give up the pendings to the seller, but keep in mind that if you do that, you're going to be paying overhead for several months with no revenue stream from the pendings. A better compromise may be somewhere in the middle, such as giving the seller half of the pendings as they close.

- *LISTINGS:* (50 to 100 percent of company dollar): As mentioned in our formula section, listings can be the sole basis of valuation — but they can also be factored in as one of the variables. Most people are willing to give up most or all of the income on listings to get the agents. Though increasingly, I'm seeing transactions in which the buyer pays 50 percent on listings and maybe an override on agents for a year.

- *SALES AGENTS/COMPANY OVERRIDES* (5 to 15 percent of company dollar): At the end of the year, you give the seller 5 to 15 percent of all the company dollars that his agents closed. This may be paid quarterly from 1-3 years.

- *BROKER'S COMMISSION SPLIT:* As part of the transaction, the broker may be offered a significantly higher percentage split for all sales made as an agent with the new company.

THE "NEED" VARIABLES

While the above negotiation tools are all essential, they are fairly standard; almost everyone uses them. Beyond these, however, you also have certain "need variables" at your disposal. These will tend to be particularly helpful tools because they're not used by everybody else. And they also tend to focus on the immediate and long-term needs of the seller, bringing you once more back into the win/win approach.

If you've done your homework at this point and understand the seller, you can use the need variables to find ways to create good will in the buyer/seller relationship, and to retain this person as a productive member of your new team. And, from a bottom line standpoint, you will end up paying less simply because you have found ways to address the seller's real needs.

The following are a few of the specific areas where you can help:

- *DEBT ASSUMPTION.* As we discussed in Chapter 5, if you can help the seller out of a financial crunch — helping to pay overdue bills — there may be tremendous benefits for everyone involved. You would assume a portion or all of the debt in lieu of purchase price.

- *EQUIPMENT RENTAL ASSUMPTION AND LEASE ASSISTANCE.* When sellers are closing down an office, they're often anxious to get out from under various leases for the building, the computer system, and so on. If you can help them deal with these leases, it's a big plus for you. In closing down an office, one approach that has been very successful for me is to agree to share in the lease expenses for six months, while offering to work together with the seller to sub-let the space to another tenant. This is usually a profitable concession monetarily and helps build a new team relationship.
- *TITLE/RESPONSIBILITIES.* Consider making the seller a vice president or senior VP to sweeten the transaction. This also allows the seller to "save face" and feel better about sell-

ing the company. The seller can now tell his/her friends at the country club that after the "merger," he/she will be a senior VP with a much larger company.

- *COMMISSION SPLITS.* If seller wants to get back to being an agent, take part of the purchase price and apply it toward giving them a higher split (that way they're earning their own payment back; they may trust themselves to earn the override back more than their agents). I would suggest paying this overage in a separate payment check tied to the purchase, so when the payments stop they will be accustomed to normal commissions.

- *OFFICE SPACE AND SECRETARIAL SERVICE.* Giving the seller a nice, professional setup at work for the next year(s) will help them to make the transition from being an owner to being an agent or manager. And you may want to hire an assistant for them, too (part-time or full-time). It is always a good idea to shift some of your purchase money into areas that will potentially generate additional revenue to the company and help you re-coup your investment more quickly.

- *INSURANCE COVERAGE.* This is very much on people's minds these days; if you offer to pick up the seller's family insurance for a year, that will create a lot of goodwill.

- *ADVERTISING ALLOWANCE.* If the seller is going to work as an agent, offer to pay a couple of hundred dollars a month for ads in the market magazine.

- *CAR PHONE.* Another way to help the broker who's selling to you make that transition back to sales. We once purchased a company for a $20,000 total investment that was probably worth 3 or 4 times that, by providing the seller with a part-time secretary, advertising and a car phone (the value of which was all included in the purchase price). This was a priority to the seller, who just wanted to get set up quickly as an agent; she said she knew how to make money as an agent.

- *OFFICE MOVING ASSISTANCE.* This may seem like a minor thing, but it could turn out to be significant. In one instance, we were acquiring a company in Georgia being sold by an older woman who was retiring. Several bidders emerged. No one wanted her office or furniture, and our buyer offered to come in with a moving truck and help her move furniture out and auction it off. He ended up with the company, paying about $10,000 less than the other bidders simply because he was concerned enough to find out what she really needed. She wanted an easy way out of her business.

- *BOARD DUES, MEMBERSHIP FEES.* As an owner, the seller was probably used to having all of this taken care of. Consider a set time frame for continuing the payments.

I can't emphasize too much the importance of these "need" variables. I've seen it time and time again. But keep one thing in mind: These are not mere "giveaways," designed just to curry favor with the seller and bring the price down. A smart seller will probably see through that kind of gimmicky, manipulative approach. YOU SHOULD REALLY BE TRYING TO INVEST IN THE SELLER'S FUTURE. Once again, you should be practicing a win/win approach, trying to find the best long-term solutions for the seller and yourself. And the interesting thing is that if you manage to do that, one of the by-products will probably be a lower price and more successful acquisition.

Having now dealt with all of the many considerations and variables and formulas, you should at this point have a sense of how much you want to pay, how you might want to pay it, and what kind of a partnership you wish to create with the seller. All the preparations, at last, are finished. Now it's time to put the deal in motion — and make an offer the seller can't refuse.

VARIABLES

Negotiating Variables

Cash upfront
Pendings
Listings
Agent/Co. overrides

Need Variables

Debt assumption
Equipment rental/ lease assistance
Title/ responsibilities
Commission splits
Office/ secretary
Insurance
Advertising allowance
Car phone
Moving assistance
Dues, membership fees
Other needs specific to the seller

Fig. 7-E

CHAPTER EIGHT

Putting the Transaction in Motion

At this point, you've established that you want to buy a specific company, and you've figured out a range of how much it's worth to you, and how you'd like to pay for it. But most of the process up to this point has been fact-finding and informal discussion between you and the seller. Now it's time to actually put an offer on the table.

This should not, however, be a simple matter of tossing out a number; rather, you should be prepared to present to the seller a clear and detailed statement of your intentions and your plans for the future of this new venture (especially their participation in it). We've talked about having a vision — now is the time when you must convey that vision, in its entirety, to the seller. Prior to this time, you have listened to the seller's needs, researched the best solutions, and are now ready to implement them with his/her help.

At the heart of this presentation will be a document known as the LETTER OF INTENT. In this chapter we will cover all of the things that should be included in that important letter. But we'll also talk, later on in this chapter, about HOW TO PRESENT YOUR OFFER TO THE SELLER — because this is the point at which the often misunderstood art of negotiation comes into play.

THE LETTER OF INTENT

Start with the letter of intent: It should be done only when you feel as if you know the seller's company like the back of your hand. But at the same time you don't want to wait too long: Don't wait until the contract stage to present a detailed explanation of your offer. (SEE SAMPLE LETTER OF INTENT, FIG. 8-A).

EXAMPLE

Johnson Realty:
1) Annual company dollar: $ 100,000
2) Net Operating Income: $ 8,000
3) Estimated Purchase Price: $ 52,000
4) Estimated Real Cost to Buyer: $ 35,000

Estimated Value of Offer:
1) Servicing the pendings: $ 10,000
2) Override: $ 20,000
3) Copier: $ 4,000
4) Health Insurance: $ 3,000
5) Personal Sales Bonus: $ 15,000
TOTAL: **$ 52,000**

TO: Johnson Realty
FROM: Jones Realty
SUBJECT: Acquisition

    It is the intent of Jones Realty to acquire certain assets of Johnson Realty. These assets are the Listing Inventory, the Independent Contractor Agreements with the Sales Associates, furniture and fixtures, and the Company Good Will. The two companies will be merged into one location at 123 Main Street, Anytown, USA.
The estimated purchase price will be $52,000.

In order to accomplish this we agree to the following:

1) All listing agreements and agent licenses will be transferred from Johnson Realty to Jones Realty.

2) Jones Realty agrees to service and close all the currently pending sales of Jones Realty at no fee.

3) Susan Johnson will become a vice-president and Senior Sales Associate with Jones Realty.

4) Susan Johnson will be paid a 10% override on the company dollar generated for the next two years on all agents that produce company dollar for Jones Realty.

5) Jones Realty will assume the lease on the Sharp copier model XX at $320 per month, currently leased to Johnson Realty.

6) Jones Realty will pay health insurance for Susan Johnson for one year.

7) Jones Realty will pay a commission of 60% on all sales personally generated by Susan Johnson, and a purchase price bonus of 10% for two years.

8) The confidentiality agreement dated June 1, 1995 will remain in effect for one year past the date of this agreement.

9) The above items may be subject to legal review.

10) The aforesaid shall be accomplished prior to and shall take effect on July 7, 1995 or this letter of intent shall become "null and void."

_____   _____
Susan Johnson   Date

_____   _____
Sam Jones   Date

Fig. 8-A

The disparity between the estimated purchase and the actual real costs is caused by the reality of the acquisition. In this case, we needed the copier, could service the pendings for an additional expense of $2,000, and factored a reduction of the override paid for the two year period. We also estimated the transaction costs to be $5,000. But the value and potential are real to the seller. This is an advantage to satisfy the needs both short-term and long-term.

If you have heard in the past companies being purchased for many hundreds of thousands of dollars or millions, it is typically done throwing every potential dollar into the estimated price available. Such as the total lease payments made to the seller for the building or override opportunities stretched out over 5, 10, or more years. The dollars quickly get very large, but also not very real.

At the simplest level, the letter of intent is a written version of your sales proposal. It's the first time you'll present the terms of the sale to the seller, and it should represent a culmination of all the discussions the two of you have had, and all the information you've compiled.

But you should also use the letter of intent as an opportunity to reinforce your vision of the new company, the new opportunity for the seller, and as a means of solving the needs and challenges of the seller. And you should cover every detail of the sale, from purchase price down to the desks and copy machine; nothing should be left open to interpretation. As a rule of thumb, the following should be addressed in the letter:

- *WHAT YOU INTEND TO PURCHASE.* Be detailed and specific. Will you assume the lease on the photocopier? Will the office staff be staying? Will you purchase the furniture, and specifically how much of it (34 desks, 6 computers, etc.) Will you assume advertising contracts?

    At this point, you should make it clear that this is an asset purchase, as opposed to a stock purchase (this should be presented as a positive to the seller, in that it will make it easier for the seller to keep the existing company charter alive for purposes of receiving payments).

- *THE TERMS.* Present your offer (the total projected purchase price) and explain how you arrived at the terms. That puts the seller in your position and shows how you intend to recoup your investment. Then specify all the terms of the purchase, including the payout schedule over one year, two years, or three, as well as specifying whether those payments are conditional based on agent retention, performance or other variables.

- *CONTRACTS.* Specify that you'll need to review all existing contracts and financial records before the closing. Be as specific as possible.

- *INDEMNITIES.* State that at the time of closing the seller must acknowledge that he has current ownership rights and no hidden liabilities, and has fully disclosed the operational and financial information accurately.

- *OTHER CONSIDERATIONS.* As you've tried to deal with the seller's needs, anything that you've agreed to provide — or not provide— should be spelled out here. That might include such extras as providing a secretary for six months, advertising or training help, and so on.

- *BOOKS/INFORMATION AVAILABLE.* Up to this point, the seller may have withheld certain financial records or documents (such as tax statements); now you need to see everything to verify and support your assumptions.

- *THE AGREEMENT.* Specify that the letter is nonbinding, so that you and the seller have a way out if the terms aren't agreeable or during disclosure you determine the proposed investment isn't appropriate given the new information you've found out.

- *THE PROJECTED CLOSING.* State exactly when the closing will occur. Depending on the companies' size, plan from two weeks to as much as three months for the transaction to close.

- *CONFIDENTIALITY.* Specify that you require complete confidentiality regarding the agreement, and plans for announcement will be mutually agreed upon or at buyer's discretion.

- *SIGNATURES.* Ask the seller to sign the letter of intent and then sign it yourself. That won't legally bind either of you, but it indicates that you're serious and agree in principle with the terms of the transaction. A large percentage (80%) of the transactions occur once the letter is agreed to.

THE BIG PRESENTATION

Once you've developed a letter of intent — either in a rough or finished form — how do you present it to the seller? I think the best way is not to hand a formal-looking letter to the seller, but rather to introduce it informally. One approach is to have the letter of intent ready, but to initially approach the seller with a notepad and perhaps some supporting documents. You might say, "I'm putting together a formal letter of intent, but first I'd like to talk it through with you. Here's what I have in mind..."

Mario Polo of the Polo Group says he prefers to combine the letter with a verbal presentation. "If you just give someone a letter of intent, it's impersonal and it also leaves open the possibility that the seller might misinterpret something in the letter," Polo says. "You have to be there telling them why it was structured the way it was — and why it's the best solution for everyone involved."

When presenting the offer, show the seller exactly how the payments will break down; i.e., you're giving the seller 10 percent upfront, 40 percent in 90 days (as pendings close), and 50 percent over the next two years (overrides on agents). Make it clear that this will assist with the seller's financial needs not just now but in the future. Also point out the items you've included to help the seller with their new career needs.

Indeed, the letter should be presented to the seller not just as an offer but as a blueprint for the future. (SEE CHECKLIST ON PRESENTING OFFER, FIG. 8-B) You should make it clear that the particular needs of the seller — i.e., the desire to become an agent again, or other goals and aspirations — have been carefully considered and worked into the proposal.

PRESENTING THE OFFER

When presenting the offer you must:

A. Re-inforce new company vision
B. Satisfy as many needs of the seller as possible
C. Express the win/win approach
D. Make it clear that your offer is a solid, "real" one (not a negotiating ploy)
E. Be willing to walk away

Fig. 8-B

PROBLEM SOLVING TIME

This is, in effect, your "problem solving meeting" — in which you're sharing with the seller that you have arrived at what seems to be the best solution to the various problems and needs of all parties involved. Among other things, the problem solving meeting should:

- Re-enforce the new company vision. Discuss the potential; where can we both go together? We can get there more quickly together and go further than we can separately. The seller can and will be a player in the future.

- Create an easy transition, by making it clear that you've addressed problems such as leases or debts or anything that might get in the way of the seller saying "yes." Plan for the "What would I do with _____?" or the "How would I _____?" questions that will be asked.

- Make it clear that this is a "serious offer" that is being presented, one that is fair and incorporates the needs of both sides. You have spent a great deal of time and energy determining the best solution. The offer must be right for both parties for the transaction to work. This is NOT a low-ball first offer or a negotiating ploy. You want to establish right away that while you're open to discussion and you want to find mutual solutions, you're not interested in haggling over the dollar figure. Instead, you're saying, "This is what I believe is fair for you and me."

    For this approach to work, you must really start out with your BEST OFFER, as opposed to an unrealistically low one. Because if you toss out an unrealistic offer, you open the gates to all kinds of bidding and negotiation and counteroffers — and once this kind of win/lose negotiation process gets start-

Putting the Transaction in Motion

ed, it's hard to stop it and you'll probably lose money and trust in the process.

It may be natural for the seller to try to put forth a counteroffer, and should be expected, but you should make it clear that this is the total amount you can reasonably pay, and that it is not simply a bid but a carefully considered and structured offer that is designed to meet everyone's needs. If a counter offer is proposed, then go back to your basic valuation premise. A restructuring of the terms could provide for a higher price or a different form of overall compensation. Use all avenues available to meet the seller's needs and yours.

Many people present a preliminary transition plan with the offer to assure the seller: 1) you really are prepared and thorough, 2) the agents will be taken care of; there is a direction, and 3) if I say yes, this will really happen, be done well, and over with soon.

- *BE WILLING TO WALK AWAY.* You may have to say, "I appreciate where you're coming from, but this is what I believe to be the best solution to our challenges." There are many variables that could be adjusted and still keep the purchase price in the same price range. (If the offer truly is a fair one, they'll probably call you back a week later and say, "let's talk again." I have seen many situations in which the seller called back a week, month, or even a year later, ready to move forward.) All good business people must at some point be able to say no and mean it. Pre-determine what your "transaction won't work" threshold is, stick to it, and profit from your experience.

TALKING TO THE AGENTS

After you've presented your offer to the seller, you may immediately want to begin talking about the transition plan. You should make it clear that as you move from the present meeting to the signing of the contract and beyond, you will need the seller's help and cooperation every step of the way. It's a good time to ask advice, i.e., "How should we best communicate this to top producers, and how might the announcement meeting be handled?" The two of you should be working on the transition plan together. And one of the very first things you'll have to decide together is when you're going to talk about all of this to the agents.

Most like to control the timing and content of the announcement as opposed to telling some key agents much earlier and the news leaking out as it almost always does. This typically causes much more concern and speculation on the agent's parts who may be hearing it "third hand." Typically, top-producing agents and key people in the seller's company will be told about the acquisition/merger THE NIGHT BEFORE you make the official announcement to everyone else. The seller may meet with these people initially for about a half-hour; immediately afterwards, you (the buyer) might meet with these same people (possibly take them to dinner with the seller) to introduce yourself and ask for their support at the next day's announcement.

The seller must ask his agents to trust his decision, and that the best interest of the agents has been carefully considered. As company leaders the other agents will look to this group for reaction to comments. The seller has hopefully earned the right to ask for a minimum of a "wait and see" attitude, if not positively optimistic support.

GIVING AGENTS A VOTE

But some buyers take a different approach. Instead of waiting until just before the announcement, they like to give advance notice of the planned acquisition/merger to all of the seller's agents — so that they can find out, early on, whether the agents approve of what's happening and support it. In some case, the agents are even given the power to vote on the acquisition.

Mark Masters of ERA Prestige Homes says that after he has presented his offer to the seller, he immediately puts the acquisition to a vote among the agents. "Having them vote on the merger is very important," says Masters. "Then, afterwards, you can say: 'I didn't just go in and buy this company — I put it up to a vote and they agreed to join me.' When you do this, you are empowering the agents by allowing them to make the decision, and that immediately builds loyalty. And you'll need that loyalty, because recruiters are going to swarm in once the acquisition is announced."

Typically, Masters requires an 80 percent approval in the vote, though in some cases, a 60 percent majority may be acceptable. Before the vote, he does a thorough presentation to the agents, to share the vision — not unlike the presentation that has already been made to the seller. Masters spends a couple of days outlining the various ways in which his support services can make the agents more productive. He brings in some of his own agents to provide testimonials to back up what he's saying. And finally he attempts to answer any questions the agents might have. "By the time I put it to a vote," he says, "I'm pretty confident that they'll vote in my favor." And if they don't? Masters says that if agents do end up voting against him, "then that means the acquisition wasn't meant to be, and they probably would have defected anyway."

Some brokers have learned that lesson firsthand. Chet Hogan of ERA Associate Realty of Indian River says that he did one acquisition in which he thought he was getting 35 agents — but only 17 actually came over. "I didn't do a vote among the agents, but if I had it to do over again, I would. You need to know that the agents you're acquiring will want to stick around."

THE TRANSITION PLAN

The period between the signing of the letter and the closing is the time to develop and coordinate a transition plan, in which you map out all the activities you need to tackle before the closing so that there'll be a smooth transition (SEE SAMPLE TRANSITION PLAN, FIG. 8-C). Never wait until after a closing to envision how and when your new company will unfold, because the result will be nonproductive time for your existing and new agents, or worse, confusion or a feeling of being in limbo, which fosters having competitors recruiting and defections. The transition plan should include the following:

- *TIME-LINE PREPARED FOR EVENTS.* Get a time sequence of everything that's going to occur, and who's responsible for making that happen and when.

- *BUDGET PREPARED.* Consider how much it's going to cost to transition a company; it's a substantial expense that people often overlook. There's a big initial cash outlay in the transition period for signs, stationary, etc. All of the new people must be converted into your culture — and it shouldn't cost them a cent.

- *MATERIALS ORDERED.* Business cards, name badges, signs and so on, should be ready for the kickoff day (usually the day after the closing). New agents will be impressed when you hand them their gift-wrapped new business cards ready to use at the announcement meeting.

- *COMMUNICATIONS WITH KEY PEOPLE.* Set a timetable of when you're going to talk to key people, whether it's a week before or a month before or the night before the actual announcement. (Unless you're allowing the agents to vote, my suggestion is to hold back on telling key people until the night before — this helps preserve confidentiality.

- *KICKOFF DAY SET.* This event is held the day the announcement is made to your key people, normally soon after the contract has been signed. Throw a major kickoff event — complete with decorations, signs, brochures, music and so on — for your new agents. The purpose is to sell your vision of the company and get everyone excited about starting fresh. Concentrate on the sizzle; save the substance for later. When new agents return to their office, you'll want to have the new company sign in place and your agents there to welcome them personally. (More details on the kickoff will be covered in the next chapter).

- *COMMUNITY IMPACT DAY PLANNED.* Typically the day after the kickoff; signs would be changed, there might be a newspaper announcement or other means of alerting the community about the "new company."

- *FIRST 90 DAYS PLANNED.* This would include implementing training and orientation programs, as well as one-on-one reviews and counseling.

- *DEVELOP NEW OFFICE POLICIES AND PROCEDURES.* Cover such items as opportunity time, postage and long-distance calls, and advertising.

- *CREATE A TRANSITION TEAM.* After the acquisition, a team with a mix of a few agents from the buyer's company and a few agents from the seller's company should help to implement new policies and programs.

- *INFORM THE COMMUNITY.* Within three days after the

kickoff, agents should notify all listers of the company change, and all promotional vehicles should be switched; letters should be sent to inform members of the real estate community of the change.

- *CREATE NEW COMPANY BUSINESS PLAN/PRO FORMA.* It's time to take the rough pro forma created earlier and fine tune it.

As you can see, the transition plan can be fairly elaborate, though it should be noted that generally a transition plan for a larger company is more difficult and costly than that of a smaller company. Obviously, it's easier to absorb five people than 50. But in any case, it's important to get started on the transition plan early, and to deal with it adequately and thoroughly.

With your letter of intent signed and your transition plan underway, the acquisition is now almost complete. But this is no time to relax. As the buzz about the impending transaction picks up, it's important to move ahead quickly... to the final stage of closing the deal and signing the contract.

SAMPLE
TRANSITION TEAM STRATEGY SESSION

1. Implementation
2. Listing Opportunities
3. Buyer Opportunities
4. New Team Member Opportunities
5. Public Relations Plan

	Date Needed	Date Ordered / Begun	Person Resp.	Completed Yes/No	Comments
1) Date					
2) Location					
3) Attendees Selected					
4) Attendees Notified					
5) ERA Attendees Notified					
6) Attendee Background Distr.					
7) Agenda					
8) Room Set-up					
9) Materials Needed					

Fig. 8-C

Sample Implementation Plan

Pre-Conversion Needs

	Date Needed	Date Ordered / Begun	Person Resp.	Completed Yes/No	Comments
1) Office Closing					
2) Human Resources Re-Allocation					
3) Equipment Re-Allocation					
4) Signs-Residential					
5) Signs-Commercial					
6) Business Cards					
7) Car Sign					
8) Bus Banners					
9) Stationery					
10) Name Badges					
11) Career Apparel					
12) Misc. Supplies					
13) Office Signage					
14) Media List					
15) Consumer Database					
16) Technology Systems Analysis					
17) Software Ordered					
18) Business Plan					
19) Pro-Forma					
20) Marketing Plan					

Fig. 8-C

SAMPLE
IMPACT DAY - COMMUNITY

	Date Needed	Date Ordered / Begun	Person Resp.	Completed Yes/No	Comments
1) Date					
2) Signs Installed Residential					
3) Signs Painted Commercial					
4) Sign Installed Commercial					
5) Press Notified					
6) Sellers Notified					
7) Advertising					
8) Open House - Agents					
9) Community Notified					
10) Service Areas Mailed					

Fig. 8-C

Sample
Impact Day - Agents

	Date Needed	Date Ordered / Begun	Person Resp.	Completed Yes/No	Comments
1) Location Selected					
2) Menu					
3) Time					
4) Agenda					
5) Speakers Briefed					
6) Materials Delivered					
7) Cards/Badges Wrapped					
8) Prizes Selected					
9) Color Photos/EIS Demo					
10) Room Set-up/AV					
11) Decorations					
12) Display					
13) Agent Packets					
14) Car Signs Changed					
15) Office Banner Hung					
16) Photographer					
17) Press Notified					
18) Seller Notification Packet					
19) Buyer Notification Packet					
20) Warranty/Referral Offer					
21) Review of Roll-Out Schedule					
22) Convention					
23) Beyond Excellence Info.					

Fig. 8-C

SAMPLE
IMPLEMENTATION - POST IMPACT DAY

	Date Needed	Date Ordered / Begun	Person Resp.	Completed Yes/No	Comments
1) Calendar					
2) Selling Skills Dates					
3) Selling Skills Location					
4) Selling Skills Materials					
5) Coordinator Training					
6) Orientation					
7) Sales Meetings Content					
8) Progress Meeting					
9) Photos MLS					
10) Special Markets					
11) Business Planning Day					
12) Transition Team/ Lunch Meeting					
13) Transition Team - 6 Mos. Schedule					
14) Past Customers Mailed					

Fig. 8-C

CHAPTER NINE

Closing the Deal

At this stage, you have, in effect, already launched your partnership with the company in question. What's left now is the formality of closing the transaction and GETTING THE CONTRACT SIGNED. But obviously that can be a very important formality.

In this chapter, we'll present a sample of a contract, and tell you some of the key things that must be included in that document. And we'll also talk about some of the important activities — such as the MERGER ANNOUNCEMENT and the "KICKOFF" — that will be taking place as the acquisition process draws to a dramatic close. This will be a hectic yet exciting period, with activity swirling all around your company. But it's no time to lose sight of the details, which become critical at this stage.

Having signed the letter of intent, you should be moving toward the contract-signing as quickly as possible. The time frame between the letter of intent and the close depends upon the size of the company. With a smaller company it could be as quick as a week, though with a larger company you'd probably need at least 45 days, to order materials and make other arrangements.

THE CONTRACT

In either case, you should have sufficient time to get your contract in order. Some who are embarking on their first acquisition may feel more comfortable hiring an attorney to create a contract for them. But keep in mind that one can end up spending many thousands of dollars on attorney fees, particularly if your attorney spends a great deal of time working on minor details in the contract.

My advice is to use an attorney more as an advisor in preparing and reviewing your contract with you. Provide him/her with the details of what you would like included. Protect yourself as best as you can, but don't spend too much time and money worrying about all the "what ifs" on paper. Remember that in business, if both parties are doing well the contract is rarely ever looked at again — if a deal goes sour, you can have the best contract in the world, and the other party may still try to break it and cause problems for you. So your best protection lies not so much in the details of the contract, but in dealing fairly with the seller, making the transaction work, and anticipating potential challenges that may come up later.

To find out what should be in a real estate acquisition contract, your most reliable source will be other brokers who have done acquisitions and created contracts. For starters, you can refer to the contracts presented here (SEE SAMPLE CONTRACT, FIG. 9-A), which has been used by real companies in real acquisitions. Once you've reviewed this and other contracts as a model, you can adapt the same elements to draw up your own rough version of a contract — and then, for safety sake, bring it to an attorney to review it. The attorney can make sure you're in compliance with local regulations (in some states, the requirements for transferring listings from one company to another are different, so you should work with a local attorney who knows real estate in your market), and can also help tailor the contract to your particular situation.

SAMPLE ASSET PURCHASE AGREEMENT

Seek legal counsel; do not use this agreement without advisement

THIS AGREEMENT is made as of the _____day of _____, 1995, between _____, a _____ corporation ("Seller"); and _____, a _____ corporation or their assigns as permitted herein ("Buyer"); and _____, sole shareholder of Seller ("Shareholder").

In consideration of the premises and the mutual covenants and agreements herein contained, the parties agree as follows:

1. Transfer of Assets. On the Closing Date hereinafter defined, Seller will convey to Buyer by Bill of Sale and Buyer will purchase and acquire all of Seller's right, title and interest in and to the following assets of Seller (the "Transferred Assets"): all of Seller's cash, pending contracts, listing agreements, telephone numbers, furniture, fixtures, and equipment listed on the attached Exhibit A; and goodwill. All assets not listed above are not being transferred hereunder. Buyer will assume no liabilities of Seller, except the lease between Landlord, Inc. and Seller on attached Exhibit B and lease between ABC Office Systems and Seller on attached Exhibit C.

2. Purchase Price. The total consideration to be paid by Buyer for the Transferred Assets shall be estimated at $50,000 (the "Purchase Price") paid as follows: $10,000 cash at closing, and $6,000 promissory note to be paid in nine equal installments of $666.66 principal plus 9% interest. The first payment is due 30 days after the closing date and payments are to be made on the same day of the month every month thereafter. This note is secured by the Company's portion of the selling company's pending commissions as of _____. The additional consideration of the closed Company

Fig. 9-A

Dollar generated by the agents of the seller's company at the time of closing, noted on Exhibit D. The first payment will be due 90 days after the closing date and payments are to be on the same day of the month every 90 days thereafter for a period of two years.

3. *Instruments of Transfer.* The sales, assignments, and deliveries to be made to Buyer pursuant hereto shall be effected by the Bill of Sale, attached hereto as Exhibit E. Any time and from time to time after the closing date, on Buyer's request, Seller will execute, acknowledge, and deliver all such assignments, and transfers, as may be reasonably required in conformity with this Agreement for the adequate assigning or transferring to Buyer of the Assets sold to Buyer as provided herein.

4. *Closing.* The Closing of the sale and transfer contemplated by this Agreement shall take place at the office of Buyer's attorney at ____ p.m. on _____, 1995. Time is of the essence.

5. *Legal, Accounting and Brokerage Fees.* Each party will bear its own expenses and fees incurred in connection with the transaction contemplated hereby, including without limitation, fees and expenses of accountants and attorneys.

6. *Warranties and Representations.*

(a) Seller hereby warrants and represents to Buyer, as of the date hereof and as of the Closing Date, as follows:

(i) Seller has good and marketable title to, and owns, the Transferred Assets to be sold, assigned and transferred hereunder, and the Transferred Assets shall be transferred to the Buyer free and clear from any and all judgments, mortgages, pledges, liens, leases, security interest, options, or other encumbrances or claims except for the listing inventory which must be approved by each property owner.

Fig. 9-A

(ii) Seller possesses all necessary power to enter into this Agreement and to consummate the transactions contemplated hereby; the execution and delivery of this agreement has been duly authorized by the sole shareholder of Seller.

(iii) Pending closing, Seller will conduct business in the ordinary course and use best efforts to preserve relationships with customers and Seller's reputation in the community; Buyer and Buyer's representatives will be allowed reasonable access during normal business hours; Seller will furnish such information concerning the business as Buyer may reasonably request.

(iv) Seller knows of no development which would materially and adversely affect the business.

(b) Buyer hereby represents to the Seller, as of the Closing Date, that:

(i) Buyer possesses all necessary power and authority to enter into this Agreement and to consummate the transactions contemplated hereby.

(ii) All information provided by Seller will be kept in strict confidence by Buyer, except for: (A) disclosures to attorneys, accountants, and financial advisers of Buyer (provided Buyer secures their agreement to hold such information in strict confidence); (B) disclosures compelled by legal process.

7. Assignment. Buyer may assign this agreement to an entity formed and owned by Buyer, but such assignment shall not relieve Buyer from personal liability for compliance with the terms and conditions of this agreement.

8. Covenant not to Compete; Cooperation. The Seller agrees that for a period of one (1) year from the Date of Closing she will keep her license with _____ will not, directly or indirectly, as owner, partner, employee, consultant or otherwise, sell or list real estate with any other company. The Buyer agrees to pay _____ the 70/30 commission split she now receives.

Fig. 9-A

The Seller further agrees not to compete with Buyer by opening a real estate brokerage firm for a period of three (3) years.

9. General Provisions. This agreement shall be executed, construed and performed in accordance with _____ law. This Agreement constitutes the entire agreement among the parties pertaining to its subject matter and supersedes all prior and contemporaneous negotiations, agreements and understandings, written or oral, or the parties in connection with it. No representation, covenant or condition not expressed in this Agreement shall affect, change or restrict this Agreement. Words used herein in the singular shall include the plural and words in the masculine shall include words in the feminine or neuter gender where text of this agreement so requires. No modification, waiver, termination, rescission, discharge or cancellation of this Agreement, shall affect the right of the parties thereafter to enforce any other provision or to exercise any right or remedy in the event of any other default, whether or not similar. This Agreement shall be binding upon and inure to the benefit of the respective parties, their heirs, executors, administrators, legal representatives, successors and permitted assigns. All provisions of this Agreement shall survive the Closing, and shall not be merged into the delivery of any documents of transfer at the Closing. Each party hereto has had equal opportunity to negotiate the terms hereof and no provision alleged to be ambiguous shall be construed for or against any party based on the identity of the draftsman of that provision. If any party defaults hereunder, then in addition to other remedies, including specific performance, the defaulting party shall reimburse the non-defaulting party for all of its costs and expenses, including reasonable attorneys' fees, incurred in enforcing this Agreement.

IN WITNESS THEREOF, each of the parties has caused this Agreement to be signed, all as of this day and year first above written.

Fig. 9-A

```
┌─────────────────────────────────────────────────────┐
│                                                     │
│  SELLER:                                            │
│                                                     │
│       By:_____          │
│                                                     │
│                                                     │
│  BUYER:                                             │
│                                                     │
│       By:_____          │
│                                                     │
│                                                     │
│                                                     │
│  PLEASE SEEK LEGAL GUIDANCE BEFORE DRAFTING AN      │
│  AGREEMENT. Any part of this agreement may not be   │
│  appropriate for your state.                        │
│                                                     │
└─────────────────────────────────────────────────────┘
```

Fig. 9-A

Here are some of the most important basic ingredients that should be in any contract:

- *WHAT ARE YOU BUYING, AND HOW ARE YOU PAYING FOR IT?* Spell out very specifically what you're purchasing (furniture, fixtures, goodwill, listings, etc.) and how you are going to pay for it (dates and amounts of deferred payments), just as you did in the letter of intent. Any other terms should be explained in detail. It's also a good idea, at this point, to apply specific dollar amounts of the purchase price toward specific assets; this will allow you to write off this amount quickly. As you can see in the sample contract shown here (SEE FIG. 9-B, CLOSEUP OF CONTRACT), out of a total purchase price of $25,000, the buyer has designated that about

$18,000 is applied directly to the purchase of furniture, listings, and supplies. That portion of the purchase price can be written off much more quickly (check with your accountant) than goodwill.

• *PUBLICITY.* It's very important to specify that the buyer has total responsibility and authority to handle any communication with the outside world and the press. I've seen acquisitions in which the seller, not the buyer, handled the publicity, and ended up distorting the information. The seller may make

---

CLOSE-UP OF CONTRACT

1) ABC Realty will pay Smith Realty approximately $25,000 for the furniture and fixtures, as identified in Exhibit A, goodwill, property management with owners consent as identified in Exhibit B, along with the present listing inventory as identified in Exhibit C, paid as follows:
   A. $3,000 on September 1, 199__.
   B. 10% of annual company dollar of agents identified in Exhibit C, paid quarterly for a period of two years beginning December 1, 199__.

2) The breakdown of the approximate purchase price of $25,000 is as follows:

A.	Furniture and fixtures	$ 6,200
B.	Listing inventory	$11,800
C.	Property management	$ 5,700
D.	Supplies	$ 1,300
E.	TOTAL	$25,000

Fig. 9-B

it look as if his company acquired yours, or may make it seem as if he is running the joint operation.

- *MAKE SURE INVESTIGATIONS SURVIVE THE CLOSING DATE.* If you find out after the acquisition closes that the seller misled you about anything, you should have the right to re-adjust the contract — and subsequently the payment amount —accordingly.

- *NON-COMPETE AGREEMENT.* This is important, because in theory the seller could collect his upfront fee and then open a new real estate company across the street and hire away your agents; in fact, the seller is the most likely person to take your new agents. With a non-compete, you're trying to put a restriction on that seller's ability to compete against you in the local real estate market for the length of the time that you're making payouts to the seller. In most courts, the non-compete is only enforceable as long as the seller is being paid a reasonable amount of compensation by you for their agreement not to compete.

- *ASSIGNMENT OF PHONE NUMBER.* This may seem like a minor detail, but it's actually critically important. If you're buying an existing company that has been in business over a year, remember that people keep marketing items and their phone books around — so you should make sure the seller's old phone number is either assigned to you or forwarded to your number. We had a case in which another company in town picked up the seller's phone number and got all the benefits of years of advertising, business cards, magnets, flyswatters, calendars — many of those promotional materials were still floating around out there in the community, with that phone number to call for a real estate need.

- *ABILITY TO DISPENSE WITH USE OF COMPANY NAME.* If you're not going to use that name, then it should be specified that the name can no longer be used in any capacity. The company can remain an active corporation that you can pay money to through the length of the payout, but cannot operate in the real estate business.

- *CONFIDENTIALITY.* Once more, we deal with the matter of confidentiality; this time, the sellers and buyers agree that they won't disclose any components of what this transaction incurred (such as how much was paid). This clause is designed to protect the next transaction that you do.

- *SELLER CAN'T ASSIGN INCOME.* This is another critical matter. In a traditional asset acquisition agreement or stock sale, the seller can assign future income to a third party — such as a company that buys the future earnings at a discounted rate. But you don't want that to happen in a real estate acquisition. Part of the reason you're giving the seller future earnings is to retain loyalty. You don't want the seller to have the ability to cash out to some accounts-receivable company; you want that person to stick around to support your efforts as an interested party.
(SEE CHECKLIST FOR CONTRACT, FIG. 9-C).

THE CLOSE

At the time you sign the actual contract, you should also sign a bill of sale; this document could be necessary if, for example, you go to the phone company and you're asked to show proof that you have the right to the company's assets (SEE SAMPLE BILL OF SALE, FIG. 9-D). And with the bill of sale and the company's

> ## CONTRACT CHECKLIST
>
> *Make sure your contract specifies:*
> - What exactly you're buying
> - Price and terms
> - How publicity will be handled
> - Assignment of phone number
> - Non-compete agreement
> - Investigations survive closing date
> - Use of company name
> - Confidentiality
> - Seller can't assign income

Fig. 9-C

assets in your possession, then you truly own that desk and those chairs — they can't be taken back from you (at least not too easily). While you're signing these documents, you may also have to sign lease agreements and assignments of equipment.

After all the papers have been signed, the assets of the company are yours — and now it's time to make sure that everyone understands what has just taken place. Before any news leaks out about the acquisition, it's important to communicate directly with all the people who are directly involved in this event — the agents and the staff.

SPREADING THE GOOD NEWS

The process of spreading the exciting news to the key people at both companies should begin the day before the merger is announced; you might want to talk to your own key people first, in the afternoon, and then devote that evening to communicating with

Sample Bill of Sale

THIS BILL OF SALE AND ASSIGNMENT is made this ____ day of _____, 1995, by and between _____, a State corporation (the "Seller") and _____ (the "Buyer").

    NOW, THEREFORE, FOR AND IN CONSIDERATION of the sum of TEN DOLLARS ($10.00) cash in hand paid and other good and valuable consideration, receipt and sufficiency of which is hereby acknowledged, the Seller hereby assigns and transfers to Buyer all of Seller's right, title, and interest in and to all of the assets of Seller as reflected on Seller's list of assets attached hereto as Exhibit A and expressly made a part hereof.

    Except as otherwise stated in the Asset Purchase Agreement dated of even date herewith, all assets are sold "as is, where is", without further warranty and Seller makes no representation or warranty as to the quantity or description of the various items of furniture, fixtures, equipment, or computers.

WITNESS the following signatures:

SELLER:

    By:_____

BUYER:

    By:_____

Fig. 9-D

the seller's key people, as we addressed in Chapter 8. It's a good idea to inform the seller's top associates, management and key personnel over a special dinner that night. Let these people know the rationale behind the acquisition. Explain what their status will be in the newly-expanded company, and to whom they will be reporting. Try to instill excitement about the opportunities ahead. Ask for their support — and if they can't provide that, ask them to at least remain neutral on the issue for a minimum of 90 days until the new company has a chance to get started.

KICKOFF TIME!

On the day of the merger announcement, or the "kickoff," you want to have everything well-planned and ready to go. (SEE PRE-KICKOFF CHECKLIST, FIG 9-E). As the day begins, two separate announcement meetings are necessary: You must announce the news within your own company, and you must also announce it to the group that is being acquired. One possible solution is to bring the two groups together. For example, one of the companies I worked with decided to hold the announcement for both groups in the same hotel; the buyer reserved two separate rooms, made the announcements separately to each group, then brought everyone together for the "new company" sales meeting/party. On hand were balloons, streamers, a band — as well as new company signs, business cards, and other support materials.

If you decide to make the announcements to the two groups at separate locations, you'd start with your group. Again, you would explain the rationale, benefits, and the history of the acquisition. As you discuss the reasons for doing the acquisition, you should de-emphasize the benefits to you as an owner (such as increasing market share or becoming more cost-efficient), and instead focus on the benefits and advantages to the people at the company, such as more

> ### PREPARING FOR KICK-OFF CHECKLIST
>
> *Prior to kickoff day, the following must be arranged:*
>
> - Arrange time and place for merger announcement
> - Have new business cards, stationery ready
> - Prepare informational "handout" for the meeting
> - Talk to key agents at both companies the day/night before (See Transition Plan, Figure 8-C)

Fig. 9-E

advertising, buyer calls, and activity. It's a good idea to have some type of handout ready, which may provide some background on the company you're acquiring and even some information about the people who are coming over to join your team.

MEETING YOUR NEW TEAM

Meanwhile, the news must simultaneously be announced at the seller's company — and the buyer's presence is required there, too. It's hard to be in two places at once, so you may want to stagger the schedule, announcing the news at your company at 8:00 in the morning, and going over to see the seller's group at 9:00. This is important: DON'T ALLOW THE SELLER TO MAKE THE ANNOUNCEMENT TO HIS COMPANY WITHOUT YOUR BEING THERE. There are two reasons for this: One, you would have no control over what the seller might say. And secondly, the seller's people are bound to have immediate questions about new policies that affect them, and you need to be there to answer their questions, and allay any anxieties.

This announcement to the seller's group should be held either at the seller's company or preferably off-premises, at a hotel. (If the acquired group is going to continue working at their current facility, then go off-premises for the meeting; that way you can change signs and make other "welcome" arrangements while they're gone). The seller should speak to the group first, but make sure that everything he says has been scripted between the two of you in advance. THIS IS AN IMPORTANT EVENT, SO PRACTICE TO MAKE SURE YOU GET THE DETAILS RIGHT. It is a time for the seller to tell his agents that an outstanding opportunity has been provided for them by bringing the two companies together. The seller is also telling them the basic facts they need to know (we'll be closing our old office on such and such a date, and moving to the new office at such and such location, etc.). But the emphasis of the seller's presentation should be to convey that he is acting in the interests of the agents and staff; he should be saying, "I truly believe this is the right way to go, trust me on this — and even if you have doubts, give us 90 days to change your mind." Theoretically, the agents trust him and they need to hear this reassuring message from him before they hear anything from you, the buyer.

SHARING THE VISION

When the seller is finished speaking, he should then introduce you to the group. The first thing to do is compliment the seller and his entire company on the outstanding job they've done over the years. Then talk about how excited you are to be bringing together this high-quality group with your own strong team. Tell the group about your vision for the new company, the various programs, and about the opportunities it holds for all of them to make more money than ever before. Add some "sizzle" to the presentation. You need to make a great first impression. A few other steps to follow at this meeting include the following:

- Share an outline of the transition plan.

- Tell the agents that their sellers will be notified about the company change through newspaper ads, signs, and direct mail.

- Let them know that you've arranged a press announcement to spread the news.

- Inform them about the transition team that is in place.

- Let them know about any training that may be scheduled.

- Tell them that new signs will be going up immediately.

- Assure them there will be no down time during the transition. In fact, you are expecting listings and sales to increase.

- Present them with gift-wrapped new business cards and stationery, a company name tag, and a listing presentation book.

- Finally, open the floor to a few questions (most should have been addressed in the presentation).

- I always advise having a couple of supportive agents coached to comment at the end, thanking the seller for all his/her support (of course it needs to be genuine) and the opportunity they have provided. Hopefully they will comment with excitement on the great potential with the new company.
    In many cases, we have had good luck getting local dignitaries and press to attend. The whole meeting should probably last between one and one-half to two hours.

After the announcement, the agents would leave the meeting and proceed to the place where they will be working (your office, if it's a fold-in). You might want to create a festive atmosphere there by hiring a band or serving champagne. Your own agents would be there to greet them. They would arrive to find that all signs have been changed to reflect the new company name. This will give the look and feeling of a brand new workplace, and should get them excited right away. Still, don't be surprised if some of your new agents seem a little detached and unenthusiastic that first day. "You don't want to force things too much that first day, because some of the agents may still be shocked and even a little angry that their company was sold," says Gloria Frazier.

COMMUNITY IMPACT

But you should try to keep building positive feelings by scheduling a party a few days after the kickoff. Gloria Frazier has, in the past, held pot luck grand opening parties; Mark Masters holds staff barbecues; Mario Polo likes to host a wine and cheese party. In any case, the idea is primarily to bring together the agents and staff in order to get to know each other and have some fun — though the party can also be used as great way to call attention to the merger in your community.

Such a "community impact" event may be open to clients, other real estate companies, and even the local press. At this point, one of your objectives should be to get as much mileage as possible out of the two groups coming together. "You're trying to make as big a splash as you can afford," says Mario Polo, who advertises his grand openings in local newspapers, some brokers will even spring for TV or radio ads to promote the big day. (SEE SAMPLE NEWSPAPER ANNOUNCEMENT, FIG. 9-F). At minimum, you should do a large mailing to clients and the entire real estate community. On this same day, you should change all signs throughout the community, and make sure the new corporate image is in place everywhere.

As you spread news of the partnership to the outside world, Polo and others say it's very important to project a positive "teamwork" image, referring to the union as a dynamic merger of two strong players, rather than an acquisition. "The message you're sending out to the community is that two great teams have come together and are going to be a major force in the market," Polo advises.

And in reality, that is exactly what is going to happen — if you are successful in bringing the two companies and cultures together. That is the final challenge that you face. And, as you'll see in the final chapter, it might be the greatest challenge of all.

Sample Newspaper Announcement

ABC Realty, Johnson Realty Merge
Staff writer John Doe

Two successful real estate firms in the area have merged, creating one of the largest independent real estate brokerages in Any County.

ABC Realty and Johnson Realty have merged and will combine offices, as Johnson Realty, at 123 Main Street, Anytown. The former offices of Johnson Realty will no longer be used.

Jane Jones has operated ABC Realty for eight years and its agents have won many awards from the Any County Association of Realtors for sales and other achievements.

"We are glad to be able to enhance the comprehensive services we have delivered to our customers and clients," said Ms. Jones of the merger. "We are delighted to be a part of the ERA (Electronic Realty Associates) network."

"In a time of large companies with hundreds of offices and thousands of agents growing larger, we decided there was a niche in the market that could most appropriately be filled by a closely held real estate firm of high quality, service-oriented Realtors who are able to deliver the comprehensive services required today by consumers," said Susan Johnson, president of Johnson Realty.

"This addition to Johnson Realty will permit our combined resources to meet all of the needs of buyers and sellers in Any County," she said.

ERA offers the Electronic Home Selling Network, an international photo multiple listing service; a home warranty program; a guaranteed sales program; one of the most comprehensive training programs available; and fully-developed buyer agency and seller agency programs, said Ms. Johnson.

The newly-merged office will have a total of about 55 agents, said Ms. Johnson. Johnson Realty, which has offices in Another Town and Any City, too, has a total of about 150 agents, counting the newly-merged Any Town office, she said.

Ms. Johnson has owned her own company for 22 years and it was recently named the second-largest woman-owned businesses in the City Metropolitan Area and the only woman-owned real estate firm in the Top 50 woman-owned business, according to the City Business Journal.

Fig. 9-F

CHAPTER TEN

Making It All Work

The contract is signed. The two teams have come together with smiles all around. The kickoff celebration was a huge success. Does this mean you've got it made? On the contrary, you've only just begun.

The ultimate success of your acquisition will be determined in the weeks and months after the papers have been signed and the welcome speeches have been delivered. It is at this point that you will begin to see how well the two sides mesh, and whether the new company can fulfill the goals that you established when you first decided to pursue an acquisition.

Horror stories abound about acquisitions that have gone sour during the honeymoon period immediately after the closing. And almost every one of those worrisome tales involves one common scenario —agent defections. Almost without exception, this can turn a successful acquisition into a failure, seemingly overnight. "If agents leave you after the acquisition, then you have lost the most important part of the whole deal," says broker Chet Hogan.

How could such a thing happen? How is it that savvy brokers sometimes get blindsided on the most critical aspect of the whole acquisition process? Often, it's a lack of follow-through on the part of the buyer. After you've gone through the acquisition process, you may be tired and think it's time to relax — but the reverse is true — you have to be more involved than ever before.

AFTER THE PARTY ENDS

What happens immediately after the acquisition is that there's a huge initial surge, with a lot of positive talk and many promises being made. The whole atmosphere in the ensuing days, as you celebrate and announce the "merger," is a festive one and it tends to build great expectations among staff and agents — as it should.

But oftentimes, as the party dies down, the broker becomes invisible. The acquired agents don't see anything to back up the talk about the new company, and about new opportunities. It goes on for a couple of weeks or maybe months, and soon agents begin saying: "This isn't what he promised."

On the other hand, sometimes the problem is not with the acquired agents but rather with the existing ones: So much time and attention has been spent on wooing and welcoming the new people that the existing agents get jealous, and start looking around.

It is imperative that you not only be attentive, but also fairminded; everything that you do for a new agent, you also must do for existing ones. With regard to agent retention, the following is one more Checklist of Considerations to Never Forget (SEE FIG. 10-A):

1) *OVERCOMMUNICATE ON EVERYTHING.* Communicate to the entire staff by memo, newsletter, voice mail, and in person. And to help foster better internal communications, you should rely on a "transition team" — composed of a few people from each side of the acquisition — to make sure agents and staff are kept informed. This could be your existing Advisory Board or President's Club, but it must include

some members from the acquired company. One part of the team may be responsible for training, another part for marketing, and another for weekly meetings.

2) *RELY ON YOUR TRANSITION TEAM.* As previously mentioned, this team is comprised of key people from both the "old" and "new" groups. The team should be assigned specific functions and duties to help smooth the transition, such as:

- Agreeing upon the length of time the team will be functioning. Pre-set regular meeting dates for a review of the process;

- Planning a social function to help bring the two sides closer;

- Looking at policies from both companies to see what should be kept and changed;

CHECKLIST OF CONSIDERATIONS TO NEVER FORGET

1) Overcommunicate on everything
2) Rely on your transition team
3) Be available
4) Work closely with the new agents
5) Don't forget your "old" associates
6) Ask for a little time
7) Don't rock the boat
8) Take the best of both companies
9) Implement great ideas
10) Take advantage of momentum

Fig. 10-A

- Reporting weekly to the broker during the first 90 days on how the transition is going and what improvements might be needed.

- Once the transition period is concluded, these people could become your "President's Council," and continue to meet on a monthly basis.

3) *BE AVAILABLE.* In fact, be more visible than you've ever been. People are going to have a lot of questions, and they're going to need guidance and leadership.

4) *WORK CLOSELY WITH THE NEW AGENTS.* The people who have been acquired may have the feeling that they've been "taken over." They may be concerned that they'll be treated like a step-child at the new company. That's why it's important to establish a one-to-one rapport with the new agents immediately. Sit down (you or your management team) with every new agent coming in and do goal planning and get to know them.

   And don't try to do all the welcoming by yourself. Says Gloria Frazier: "It's a good idea to pull together your best team players from the old company and say, 'We've got to make these new people feel like part of the group — so I'd appreciate it if you'd take some of these people out to lunch and do anything you can to help.'" You might consider using a "MENTOR" PROGRAM, which would pair each "new" agent with an agent from the original group. Also, Frazier says she tries to spread the new agents throughout the office, as opposed to having them all sit together. "Anything you can do to break down the barriers is good," she says.

5) *MEANWHILE, DON'T FORGET YOUR 'OLD' ASSOCIATES.* As you spend time indoctrinating the agents, the existing ones may become resentful. Make sure they understand that they're

still part of the core team. Spend equal time with them.

6) ASK FOR A LITTLE TIME. Not everyone is going to be thrilled about the changes taking place, but you should ask everyone — even the obvious naysayers — to at least try to remain neutral for the first 90 days. "We don't want anybody — even non-performers — to leave in the first 90 days," says one broker with a top franchise chain, who has acquired several companies. The reason, he says, is that if some people start leaving, others may be tempted to follow them. So make a reasonable request of all the agents: "Don't pass judgment until you've given the new company a sufficient amount of time; you won't truly know if this system works until you try it out."

7) *DON'T ROCK THE BOAT.* Almost any radical change that you make — even if it's an improvement — could be perceived as negative, and could give people an excuse to say, "Uh-oh, here it comes." Mario Polo says that he tries "to give the agents whatever policies and benefits they've been used to, at least initially — the idea is to slowly merge them into your system and your policies." So you should be willing to give the agents the option of staying with their old policies for a while, perhaps even a year — but you should also make a strong case that they should try it your way, just to see if they like it better.

For example, your policy on splits may differ from that of the acquired company; their split may have been higher, while your company provides more service. A good approach is to say: "Try it my way for a while, and if you're not making more money with this company, then we'll revisit it — but I believe my agents earn more than what you've been used to because we provide more service."

Often, a willingness to compromise is necessary with commissions, because "if you force new splits on the agents, you may lose them," says Mario Polo. But it's also important to try to show the advantages to the agents of your policies as much as possible, because you don't want a lot of new agents getting "special treatment" on their commissions; if that happens, you'll end up having to do the same for your existing agents to be fair.

8) *TAKE THE BEST OF BOTH COMPANIES.* You'll probably get the best results if you can find a way to integrate parts of each culture into your "new" company. No matter how successful you've been, there are bound to be things that the acquired company did better than you. Don't be afraid to admit that, and to change some of your old policies.

9) *IMPLEMENT GREAT IDEAS.* If you were ever going to do something, now is a good time to do it. You have more energy and more strength than you've ever had. It's a good time to figure out new solutions to old problems, such as how incoming calls are handled, floor system, sales meeting attendance, etc.

10) *TAKE ADVANTAGE OF MOMENTUM.* With the infusion of energy and new blood, it's a great time for sales contests. For example, you might hold a one-day "telethon" in which agents call up past customers, clients and prospects to tell them about the new merger; give prizes to agents who make the most calls, with separate prizes for anyone who manages to set up sales or listing appointments or recruiting interviews.

WHEN THE HONEYMOON IS OVER

If you acquire 20 agents, you need to give everyone a chance... but at the end of 90 days if you've got four or five people who aren't fitting in with the culture, it's very important to bring them in and say — "we tried, but it's not working out" — and let go of that group. It is a positive message to everyone else that you are upholding the company's standards, and that you are willing to weed out the non-players in order to keep the company, as a whole, much stronger.

"One thing I learned from experience is that you can't let the naysayers hang around for too long," says Gloria Frazier. "I think after the first month, you have to bring these people into your office and say, 'It's time to fish or cut bait.' That can be difficult, but you have to do it. Because these people will cause problems if you let them; they're always griping about 'the way things used to be,' and that negative attitude can spread to others."

But if you let go of the bad apples, make sure you don't needlessly worry others about their security. The way to allay anxieties as you do this is through individual one-on-one meetings, in which you might say: "I'm really pleased with your efforts and progress. It's great having you on the team." After 90 days, the good players should have had a couple of those meetings, so they'll know they're really on the team and they won't be worried when they see you letting go of the non-players. In fact, they're more likely to say, "I wish our broker had gotten rid of that guy a long time ago."

You also may find that you have to let go of some members of your old team, because these people just can't accept the changes and the growth. That's understandable; not everyone wants to be with an aggressive, up-and-coming company. Some would rather be in a more laid-back, comfortable environment without change. You might have to point this out, and advise such people that "maybe you should consider moving to a company that isn't building for the future and as performance-oriented as this one." (Haven't you always wanted to be able to say this?)

Making It All Work

A GOOD TIME TO RECRUIT

As you begin to weed out a few (hopefully not too many) of these people, there will be opportunities to bring in more new people. Actually, the post-acquisition period is an outstanding time to recruit. In some ways, you're already in the recruiting mode, because you've had to recruit the acquired agents and re-recruit your own people. And at the same time, you're on a roll, with momentum and excitement... so it's a great time to springboard into a recruitment effort. And don't forget that the 10-step acquisition process that was introduced in Chapter 1 also applies very well to recruiting — from seeking out qualified candidates, to making the call, to needs analysis, and so forth. (SEE RECRUITING CHECKLIST, FIG. 10-B). That same "win/win" philosophy we've advocated for acquisitions is just as critical in successful recruiting.

HOW THE 10 STEP ACQUISITION CHECKLIST CAN ALSO BE APPLIED TO RECRUITING

1) Identify quality associates
2) Establish contact
3) Build relationship with candidate based on needs
4) Gather information
5) Determine "potential fit" of agent with your culture
6) Create a compensation program
7) Transition process
8) Mutual commitment
9) Agent integration/ retention
10) Return to step one

Fig. 10-B

STARTING OVER

Speaking of the 10-step checklist, you may recall that the last step was: "Evaluate and Return to Step One and Begin Anew." And that's what you are ready to do now. The 10th step in the process is actually a time to reflect and evaluate. What did you like about the process, and what did you have trouble with? In what areas do you think you might need to improve next time? (SEE FIG. 10-C, SELF-EVALUATION REPORT CARD)

Generally speaking, once you've successfully completed your first acquisition, you will be much better prepared for the next one. "It definitely gets easier as you move from one transaction to the next," says Gloria Frazier. "With each acquisition, you learn from experience about how to assimilate the different personalities, what to say or not say. The first time out, you'll probably make some mistakes — but if you can make it through that, you'll have a lot of confidence as you look to your second acquisition."

And make no mistake about it, you will move onto other acquisitions. Once you've done a successful acquisition, you will probably begin to view yourself as a growth-minded market leader — and thinking about acquisitions will come naturally to you. Aside from the tangible benefits of acquisitions — adding size and market share, and acquiring a team of experienced, high-quality agents — there are other underlying benefits of having succeeded at acquisitions. A company that has done it just feels differently about itself, brokers say. "It gives you a feeling of confidence and that confidence is felt by all your agents," says Mario Polo. "Everyone begins to feel that, 'We're going to take this market by storm.'"

It also changes the way that your company is perceived by others. "The residual effect is that now other real estate companies know you are capable of doing this, and it sets you apart in terms of the way you're perceived by other brokers and agents in your market," says Gloria Frazier.

Indeed, once you have gone through the entire 10-step acquisition process — from finding candidates, to building a relationship, to making that tough first call, to gathering information, to evaluating a company, to making an offer, to closing the transaction, and finally making the transition work — you have accomplished something pretty significant. Pat yourself on the back. But don't spend too much time resting on your laurels. The fact is, there are some 70,000 potential candidates out there in the real estate market right now — and many of those companies would make a good and profitable partner for a company just like yours. So what are you waiting for? Go back to Step One, and get started!

POST ACQUISITION SELF-EVALUATION REPORT CARD

(Now that the acquisition is completed, grade yourself on the following areas; A = outstanding, B = good, C = need improvement)

	A	B	C
Initial approach	✓		
Relationship building		✓	
Valuation of company		✓	
Presentation of offer			✓
Handling of announcement/kickoff			
Integration of new agents			
Areas to improve			
Methods to retain agents			

Fig. 10-C

Addendum A

CASE STUDY — "MOVE-IN" ACQUISITION

I. Needs and Objectives

BUYERS' NEEDS AND OBJECTIVES: ABC/Williams Associates (the buyer) is a 48-agent, 3-office company with sales of $57,000,000, that is part of a large national franchise operation, ABC Associates. Broker Tom Williams has a strong hold on the west side of his market, but would like to gain a stronger presence on the east side. Overall, his goals include the following:

1) To quickly increase the number of agents, without having to undertake a lengthy recruiting program.
2) Increase sales presence overall in the marketplace.
3) Looking to gain a strong presence in adjoining "east side" market; Williams already has several agents working there and currently listing inventory in that target market.
4) Wants a separate branch office in this market — but doesn't want to undertake the costs or spend the time necessary to open an office from scratch.
5) Wants to take better advantage of services offered through his franchise network, including a strong agent training program, management training programs, and a high-visibility marketing program.

SELLER'S NEEDS AND OBJECTIVES: Friendly Real Estate (the seller) is a 17-agent, single-office firm with sales of $15,300,000.

Broker Bill Friendly has seen company sales level off in the last couple of years, though his company maintains a strong operation

on the east side of town, with a good reputation for customer service. Friendly's needs are as follows:
1) Needs for his company to be much larger, much more visible in order to effectively compete in the marketplace.
2) Need for company to become more profitable.
3) Needs a better training program for agents.
4) Needs better advertising to compete with high-profile bigger competitors, such as ABC/Williams.
5) Wants his agents and staff to be taken care of.
6) Would like to continue to manage his group of agents, and to protect the strong company reputation that he's built up over the years.

QUESTIONS TO CONSIDER: Does a "move-in" make sense for ABC/Williams? If so, why? Considering Friendly's needs, what would be the advantages of joining forces with a larger operation? And what kind of role might Bill Friendly play in the new company?

II. Available facts about Seller (Friendly Real Estate)

1) Balance sheet as of Sept. 30, 1994 shows:
   - Total assets $ 169,000
   - Total liabilities $ 132,000
   - Total stockholder's equity $ 37,000
2) Profit & Loss Statement, year end, shows:
   - Total Revenues $ 474,000
   - Total Commissions Expense $ 289,000
   - Company Dollar $ 185,000
   - Total Expenses $ 179,000
   - Net income (loss) before taxes $ 6,000
   - Seller's adjusted NOI $ 17,000
3) Listing inventory current:
   - 105 listings, gross amount $ 13,125,000

- Average list price $ 125,000
4) Pending sales
  - 9 pendings
  - Total company dollar $ 13,500
5) Agents
  - 21 licensees
  - 17 full-time, 4 referral agents
  - Average split — 61 percent
6) Facility
  - 20 desks
  - 2 computers
  - Current rate $15 per sq. ft
  - 4 years remaining on lease

III. Company Valuation: Friendly Real Estate

Based on available information on Friendly Real Estate, the following valuation formulas were applied by Williams.

BOOK VALUE FORMULA: Total book value of Friendly's building, furniture and fixtures, office equipment, listing inventory and pendings equals $35,000; using current market going rate, Williams multiplies book value by two and comes up with a total of $70,000.

REPLACEMENT VALUATION: Williams estimates that it would cost approximately $75,000 to build and staff a branch office from scratch in Friendly's market.

PER AGENT: In previous acquisitions, Williams ended up paying an average of $4,000 per agent; in the case of Friendly, 17 agents would be acquired. Therefore, per-agent valuation for company based on historical acquisitions would be $68,000.

INCOME FORMULA A: Williams multiplied Friendly's adjusted net pretax earnings — $17,000 — by four to six times, resulting in a valuation range of $68,000 to $102,000.

INCOME FORMULA B: Using an annual net multiplier of three to four, Williams applies that multiplier to Friendly's earnings before interest and tax ($17,000) and ends up with a value range of $51,000 to $68,000.

INCOME FORMULA C: Williams bases value on a percentage of Friendly's annual company dollar, which amounts to $185,000. Using a range of 25 to 50 percent, that results in a company value range of $46,000 to $92,000.

QUESTIONS TO CONSIDER: Why would the "book value" and "replacement valuation" formulas be more valid than in the fold-in case study, given that this is a move-in acquisition? Why would the "per-agent" formula be less valid? Why might income formula C — based on company dollar — still tend to be the most reliable of all the valuation formulas in this situation?

FRIENDLY REAL ESTATE VALUATION RANGES:

Book Value	$70,000
Replacement Value	$75,000
Per Agent	$68,000
Pre-Tax	$68,000-102,000
Net-Multiplier	$51,000-68,000
Company Dollar	$46,000-92,000
Estimated Value	**$65,000-75,000**

IV. *The Offer*

1) Estimated Total Purchase Price: $70,000-80,000

2) Cash down... $5,000
3) Terms ... paid out over 3 years, 10% overrides of company $ on agents listed in Exhibit A.
4) Parameters of Acquisition:
Asset purchase of certain assets, excluding:
Signage
Miscellaneous supplies
Liabilities included:
> Lease
> Office Equipment (leased)
> Short-term debt (unpaid phone bill)

5) Variables:
A. Pending contracts: Williams paid Friendly 100 % of all pendings at the time of contract closing that closed in first 6 months.
B. Bonus: A pre-arranged bonus to be paid to Friendly after one year if 80 % of agents remain with company and achieve certain production levels.
C. Serviced and closed pending sales.

6) Need Variables
A. Provided Bill Friendly with executive title and responsibility to manage and oversee branch office
B. Board membership fees for Friendly are paid by Williams.
C. Health insurance for Friendly paid by Williams.

QUESTIONS TO CONSIDER: What's the advantage for Williams in paying less upfront cash, and tying subsequent payments to overrides on company dollar? Why should Williams keep Friendly on as a vice president and branch manager, instead of bringing in his own manager?

V. One Year Later: Status Report

1) Agents: retained 8 agents from Friendly Real Estate. Hired 11 additional agents.
2) Total company dollar revenues generated by branch office: $205,000
3) Listing inventory: 143 listings, value of $20,020,000
4) Operating statement
   NOI $8,000
   Budget for 1996 $21,000 NOI
5) Estimated out of pocket expenses to purchase: $24,000
   Return on investment to date   33 %
   Return forecast   40 %

QUESTIONS TO CONSIDER: After one year, does this appear to be a successful acquisition? If so, what is that judgment based on?

	Seller	*Williams Branch*	*Williams Branch*
		One Year Later	Two Years Later
Agents	17	19	23
Listings	105	143	157
Volume	$13,125,000	$20,020,000	$22,608,000
Company $	$185,000	$215,000	$241,000
Expenses	$179,000	$197,000	$207,400
NOI	$6,000	$18,000	$34,000

Addendum B

CASE STUDY — "FOLD-IN" ACQUISITION

I. NEEDS AND OBJECTIVES

BUYERS' NEEDS AND OBJECTIVES: James Wilson Realty (the buyer) is a 20-agent, single-office firm with sales of $22 million. Broker James Wilson has a profitable growing operation, but wants to accomplish the following:
1) Quickly increase the number of agents, without having to undertake lengthy recruiting program.
2) Increase sales presence in the marketplace.
3) Make better use of the Wilson headquarters facility, which has capacity to accommodate up to 30 agents.
4) Maximize the cost-efficiency of current advertising and training programs.
5) Take better advantage of Wilson's existing strong management and administrative support personnel.
6) Not looking to spend a lot of cash.

SELLER'S NEEDS AND OBJECTIVES: Hawkins & Co. Real Estate (the seller) is a 12-agent, single-office firm with sales of $10 million. Broker Ed Hawkins has seen company sales level off in the last couple of years, though his company maintains a strong operation with a good reputation in the market. Hawkins' needs are as follows:
1) Needs for his company to be much larger, much more visible in order to effectively compete in the marketplace.
2) Need for company to become more profitable.
3) Personally, wants to make more money than he's been taking out of the company in the last couple of years (would like to buy a summer cottage on the lake).

4) Wants to spend less time managing.
5) Wants his agents and staff to be taken care of.
6) Would like to somehow protect the strong company reputation that he's built up over the years.

QUESTIONS TO CONSIDER: Does a "fold-in" make sense for Wilson? If so, why? Considering Hawkins' personal goals and needs, what are some of the ways that Wilson might be able to accommodate those needs?

II. Available Facts About Hawkins & Co. (Seller)

1) Balance sheet as of Sept. 30, 1994 shows:
   - Total assets $ 88,000
   - Total liabilities $ 114,000
   - Total stockholder's equity $ <26,000>
2) Profit & Loss Statement, year end, shows:
   - Total Revenues $ 283,000
   - Total Commissions Expense $ 171,000
   - Company Dollar $ 112,000
   - Total Expenses $ 126,000
   - Net income (loss) before taxes (P&L) $ <14,000>
   - Adjusted Pre-tax $ 8,000
3) Listing inventory current:
   - 72 listings, gross amount $ 7,272,000
   - Average list price $ 101,000
4) Pending sales
   - 12 pendings
   - Total company dollar $ 16,000
5) Agents
   - 15 licensees
   - 11 full-time, 4 part-time
   - Average split — 60 percent

6) Facility
- 20 desks
- 2 computers
- Current rate $14 per sq. ft
- 2 years remaining on lease

7) Asking price
- $150,000 ... cash.

III. Company Valuation: Hawkins & Co.

Based on available information on Hawkins & Co., the following valuation formulas were applied by Wilson.

BOOK VALUE FORMULA: Not applicable, since Wilson was not buying building and other major assets.

REPLACEMENT VALUATION: Not applicable in a fold-in.

PER AGENT: In previous acquisitions, Wilson ended up paying an average of $3,000 per agent; in the case of Hawkins, 12 agents would be acquired. Therefore, per-agent valuation for company based on historical acquisitions would be $36,000.

INCOME FORMULA A: Wilson multiplied Hawkins adjusted net pretax earnings — $8,000 — by four to six times, resulting in a valuation range of $32,000 to $48,000.

INCOME FORMULA B: Using an annual net multiplier of three to four, Wilson applies that multiplier to Hawkins earnings before interest and tax ($8,000) and ends up with a value range of $24,000 to $32,000.

INCOME FORMULA C: Wilson bases value on a percentage of

Hawkins' annual company dollar, which amounts to $112,000. Using a range of 25 to 50 percent, that results in a company value range of $28,000 to $56,000.

QUESTIONS TO CONSIDER: Why would the "book value" and "replacement valuation" be less valid, given that this is a fold-in acquisition? What are the limitations of using a "per-agent" formula based on historical data? Why might income formula C — based on company dollar — tend to be more reliable than the other two income formulas, based on net earnings?

IV. The Offer

1) Cash down... $2,000
2) Terms ... paid out over 3 years, 5% overrides of company $
3) Parameters of Acquisition:
    Asset purchase of certain assets, excluding:
      Building
      Signage
      Miscellaneous supplies
    Liabilities included:
      Half of lease obligation
      Office Equipment (leased)
      Short-term debt (unpaid phone bill)
4) Variables:
A. Listings: Wilson paid Hawkins 10 percent of company dollar of all listings that sold and closed in first 6 months; paid 5 percent of listings that closed after 6 months up to to 12 months.
B. Pending contracts: Wilson paid Hawkins 75 % of all pendings that closed in first 6 months.
C. Bonus: A pre-arranged bonus to be paid to Hawkins after one year if 80 % of agents remain with company and

achieve certain production levels.
5) Need Variables
   A. Provided Ed Hawkins with office, part-time secretary at Wilson Realty (estimated value, $3,000)
   B. Ed Hawkins given higher commission split 65 % as agent with Wilson Realty
   C. Paid moving costs for Hawkins & Co. of $1,000.

QUESTIONS TO CONSIDER: What's the advantage for Wilson in paying less upfront cash, and tying subsequent payments to overrides on company dollar? Why should Wilson provide Hawkins with an office and secretary, or a higher commission split?

V. One Year Later: Status Report

1) Agents: retained 8 agents from Hawkins & Co. Hired 6 additional agents.
2) Total company dollar value of sales generated by acquired agents: $100,000.
3) Listing inventory: 256 listings, value of $27,794,000.
4) Operating statement
   NOI $32,000
   Budget for Year 2: $77,000 NOI
5) Estimated out of pocket expenses to purchase:
   1st Year: $37,000
   Return on investment to date: 59 %
   Return forecast: 100+ %

QUESTIONS TO CONSIDER: After one year, does this appear to be a successful acquisition? If so, what is that judgment based on?

	Current Situation		1 Year Later
	Buyer	*Seller*	*New Company*
Agents	20	12	30
Listings	141	72	256
Listings Volume	$15,510,000	$7,272,000	$27,794,000
Sales Volume	$22,000,000	$10,000,000	$38,400,000
Company $	$286,000	$126,000	$486,000
Expenses	$276,000	$126,000	$486,000
NOI	$10,000	<$14,000>	$34,000

Glossary of Terms

ACQUISITION: Technically, it means one company taking over controlling interest in another company. But an acquisition can and should be viewed as a mutually beneficial arrangement in which the seller willingly agrees to give up control of the company to the buyer in exchange for something the seller needs — whether it be cash or other incentives.

AGGRESSIVE APPROACH: A conventional short-term win/lose negotiating approach, in which the buyer's primary objective is to acquire a company at the lowest possible cost.

ANNUAL COMPANY DOLLAR: The gross income of a real estate company after agents have been paid.

ANNUAL NET MULTIPLIER: Used as part of a valuation formula, the ANP is equal to the inverse of the capitalization rate (i.e., if capitalization rate is 25 percent or one-fourth, annual net multiplier would be four).

ASSET SUMMATION APPROACH: A valuation formula that attempts to estimate and add up the total market value of all company assets, including tangible assets (building, furniture, listings) and intangible assets such as goodwill and quality of agents.

ASSIGNMENT CLAUSE: A clause in a lease that specifies whether that lease can be assigned to or extended to include another party; the clause may specify that an assignment fee be paid in order to transfer the lease.

COMMUNITY IMPACT DAY: An event held immediately after an acquisition is completed, usually for purposes of "introducing" the new, merged company to clients, the press, and the local community; event may include a party open to the public, sign-changings throughout the community, and a media campaign.

CONFIDENTIALITY AGREEMENT: A written agreement between buyer and seller stipulating that all information exchanged during conversations prior to the acquisition will be kept in strict confidence between buyer and seller.

CULTURE: The overall attitude, approach and philosophy of a company. The culture of a company is often determined by the broker, who attracts agents and staff with a similar attitude. A company's culture is usually evident in the relationship between agents, as well as in the way the company interacts with the public.

DEFERRED PAYMENT: Payment that is made to the seller over an extended period of time after the acquisition, usually at pre-determined payment stages.

FIXED COSTS: A cost that remains constant regardless of sales volume or number of agents; includes rent on the building, costs of furnishing the office, telephone system, and other "overhead" costs.

FOLD-IN: An acquisition in which the buyer closes down the seller's existing operation, and then folds the seller's agents (and perhaps staff and management) into the buyer's company.

HIDDEN VARIABLES: Negotiating variables that are not commonly used, and which tend to focus on the needs of the seller (i.e., assuming seller's debt, or providing seller with a title or office at new company).

IMMEDIATE (SHORT TERM) NEEDS: The needs of the seller that must be addressed right away (usually in 30 days or less), such as debt, unpaid bills, etc.

IMPLEMENTATION PLAN: See "Transition Plan."

KICKOFF: The event at which the companies of the buyer and seller are brought together for the first time and the acquisition or merger is officially announced. Typically takes the form of an announcement meeting, followed immediately by a celebration involving all agents and staff of both companies.

LETTER OF INTENT: A written proposal to buy a company, presented to the seller just prior to the acquisition. The letter usually specifies price and terms desired by the buyer, and includes other significant details. It should also reinforce the buyer's plans and vision for the future of the company.

LISTING INVENTORY: All of the property listings that a real estate company and its agents have under agreement; the company's exclusive rights to sell those properties can be considered as one of the company's transferable assets during an acquisition.

LONG TERM NEEDS: The needs of the seller with regard to his/her long-range goals and aspirations, i.e. planning the rest of their career.

MERGER: A combination of two companies through a pooling of interests. The primary difference from an acquisition is that in a merger the seller usually maintains some level of shared ownership in the new company, often through a stock transfer.

MOVE-IN: An acquisition in which the buyer assumes the existing operation of the seller, including the facility. Typically, the seller's offices, agents and staff are kept in place, and the buyer moves in and changes the signs (and may or may not install new management, agents and/or policies).

NEEDS ANALYSIS: The process in which the buyer attempts to consider and analyze all the needs of the seller.

NEGOTIATING VARIABLES: Commonly-used bargaining chips that can be offered to a seller and can be used to raise or lower the purchase price accordingly; (i.e., paying cash upfront, paying seller a percentage of pendings as they close, etc.)

OWNER COMPENSATION: The various means by which a broker/owner is paid or otherwise rewarded by his/her own company; can take the form of salary, percentage of sales, commission draw or other payment, and can also take the form of hidden "perks," such as a company car or a paid vacation.

PASSIVE APPROACH: Rather than seeking out and contacting specific candidates, a buyer using the passive approach puts out the word that he/she is interested in acquisitions, or maybe an ad in the paper — then waits for candidates to respond.

PENDINGS: Sales of real estate properties that are under contract but have not yet gone to closing.

P&L STATEMENT: Profit-and-loss statement, also referred to as financial statement, which shows company revenues and expenses on monthly and/or annual basis.

PRO FORMA: The best estimate of what a company's revenues and expenses will be for a given time period in the future.

POTENTIAL FIT: An attempt to judge, in advance, whether two companies are compatible and if they would blend well together in a merger. Review operational and cultural compatibility during the process.

RELATIONSHIP BUILDING: The development of a rapport

between buyer and seller based on mutual trust and respect.

REPLACEMENT VALUATION: A valuation formula in which the buyer attempts to estimate how much it would cost to duplicate or recreate the seller's company if the buyer were to start from scratch — building a new facility, recruiting and hiring new agents, etc.

RISK-SHIFTING: A process in which a buyer structures the terms of an acquisition so that the buyer's risk is shared between buyer and seller; in a typical risk-shifting equation, the buyer's purchase price can increase as more and more risk is shifted to the seller.

SAVING FACE: Helping the seller to maintain a sense of pride and accomplishment even as he/she is selling the company, as well as after the company is sold.

SELLING THE VISION: Convincing the seller that you have a strong plan for the future of the two companies working together.

SPLITS: Referring to commission splits, or the percentage of a real estate sale that is paid to the agent who made the sale.

SUPPORT SERVICES: Services provided by the broker that assist the agents and help them to be most productive, i.e., training courses, marketing programs, office computer system, etc.

TARGET LIST: A list of companies that would be considered ideal acquisition candidates; a buyer usually ends up with a target list of a handful of companies after considering many others.

TRANSITION PLAN: A plan developed by the buyer before the actual purchase of the company, which maps out all activities and steps that will be necessary at the time of closing and immediately afterwards (also referred to as the "implementation plan").

TRANSITION TEAM: A core team of managers, agents and/or staff, assembled prior to or at the time of closing, whose responsibility is to help ensure a smooth transition period immediately after the acquisition.

UNDERLYING NEEDS: The needs of the seller that may be hidden or not openly discussed; these can include agency defections, personal problems, etc.

UPFRONT PAYMENT: Payment (usually cash) that is made to the seller at the time of the acquisition.

VALUATION FORMULA: Any of a number of existing, established formulas that can help a buyer to determine how much a company is worth; such formulas usually provide a rough estimate or value range, as opposed to a precise number.

WIN/WIN APPROACH: A philosophy toward business dealings — and, in particular, negotiations between two companies — which stresses that both parties must benefit and be satisfied if a deal is to be successful ultimately. Runs counter to traditional approaches, which tend to view negotiations as a win-or-lose situation.